BE A CAMPAIGNER!

Animal rights and vegan campaigning is the only hope for the world.

Do you want to get active and save animals? Usually, what stops people from getting active is lack of knowledge and contacts, but we can help! We've been up and down the country talking to activists and doing it ourselves and in this book we tell everything we've learned.

By the end of this book you'll know how to set up a campaigning local group, raise money, get onto local radio and into the papers, produce newsletters and run street stalls. You'll be able to get veggie and vegan food into your work or college canteen, set up a display in your local library and organise a demonstration.

You'll be all geared up for running a public meeting or giving a school talk and if you should find yourself intimidated or arrested by the long arm of the meat industry's protectors in the cause of your legitimate activism, we'll tell you the score.

Animal rights activism spreads through personal contact. You can make it spread in your area. As tens of thousands more get active, we can look forward to a cruelty free, animal-friendly vegan country.

In our lifetimes.

- Alex

Animal abuse is widespread and upsetting, but you can be a catalyst for change.

The main reason that so much animal cruelty is happening today is because caring people don't know what they can do about it! There are countless things that you can do to campaign against cruelty, from simply handing out leaflets to organising a national demonstration. Whatever your skills and confidence, there is bound to be a way of campaigning that suits you and fits in with your lifestyle.

Whether you are an eager letter-writer, an 'out there on-the-streets' demo veteran or a college kid trying to get your canteen to serve more cruelty-free food, you will find your niche and discover ways in which you can best use your unique and very special talents.

Actively campaigning might seem like a daunting thought at first. I remember feeling frustrated when I first got involved in animal rights because I was eager and willing to do things, but totally unsure how. We all have to start somewhere and Alex and I hope that the advice and information in this book will help motivate and inspire you.

- Ronny

CONTENTS

Be a Campaigner!   Important introductory info.   1

1. Animal Rights Begins On Your Plate   15

2. Setting Up A Local Group   23

3. Initiating And Running A Local Campaign   33

4. Producing Leaflets And Posters   49

5. Street Stalls   55

6. Organising a Public Meeting   61

7. The Media   67

8. Newsletters   81

9. Displays   93

10. Speaking To Schools And Other Groups   99

11. Promoting Vegan Food   105

12. Fundraising   117

13. The Long Arm of the Law   123

14. Let's Change The World   133

15. The Campaigner's Hit Parade   147

16. Resources   151

17. And finally...   About the Authors   185

Campaign Against Cruelty
- An Activists' Handbook

Authors: Alex Bourke and Ronny Worsey

Illustrations by Ronny and Clare

First published as a set of information sheets February 1998

This new paperback edition **June 2001**. **ISBN 1-898462-02-X**
Published by **Scamp Media**, a division of Vegetarian Guides.
Front cover illustration by Mark Halunga, markmail@chello.se
Cover design, Marion Gillet, mariongb@hotmail.com

Alex and Ronny assert the moral right to be identified as the authors of this
work, with the following exceptions:
chapter 9, based on an article by Sigrid de Leo
chapter 11, case study based on an article from *Vegetarian Times*
Thanks to Neil Lea for his inspiration and suggestions for chapter 12.
chapter 13 by Tim Walker of Walkers Solicitors

This book online at www.CampaignAgainstCruelty.co.uk

Italian version at www.freeweb.org/animal/bacheca_animalista/manuale
Swedish edition will be published by Animal Rights Sweden, contact
info@djurensratt.org
Other languages in preparation, contact us for details if you can help

Printed by Cox & Wyman, Reading

Why Animal Rights is such an Important Issue

The scale of the problem

Animals suffer at the hands of humans for a wide range of reasons. Many industries have been founded on animal suffering, from the obvious ones such as farming, fishing, bloodsports, vivisection and circuses, to the more subtly cruel ones such as horse and dog racing and the pet trade.

Animals are eaten, skinned, imprisoned, tortured, trapped, degraded and persecuted by billions of different people in every country in the world. Their homes are destroyed by pollution, road building, agriculture and global warming. Entire species and their habitats are being wiped out every year, many never to be replaced.

Animal ingredients find their way into a wide range of products, such as soap, rubber, paint and candles. You only have to switch on a television or walk around a supermarket to see the overwhelming scale of the problem, but don't despair!

Our generation have a wider and easier access to facts than people ever did in the past. We can therefore be armed with knowledge more easily.

People living today have greater rights and freedoms than ever before. We have more ability to make choices about where we want to go and what we want to do. Having this access to knowledge and this freedom of choice means that we also have a greater responsibility for our decisions and actions than previous generations ever did.

You can play a very significant role in helping other people to live their lives with more responsibility for other creatures. Whichever way you choose to campaign, do it with love, pride and determination.

The Scale of the Solutions

* Vegetarian and vegan products are the fastest growing sector of the food industry.

* Between two and five thousand people turn vegetarian every week. A large proportion of them stay veggie and an increasing number progress to veganism. One in four groups of people eating out now contains at least one vegetarian. This represents huge consumer power.

* More children are being brought up vegetarian and vegan than ever before and vegetarianism and animal rights issues are on the National Curriculum which is taught in schools.

* Large companies which make money from breeding animals for experiments have been closed due to adverse publicity and animal rights campaigns in recent years and others are on the verge of closure at the time of going to print.

* British polititians have voted for a ban on hunting with hounds (although it has not become law at the time of going to print) and fur farming has now also been banned here.

* Active new groups are springing up in parts of the world which have not had a strong animal rights presence until recently. Many groups are sharing ideas at gatherings and via the internet and trying out new tactics.

* We are in the midst of a communications revolution and issues such as ethics, identity and globalisation have a much greater priority than ever before. The internet has enabled even the poorest people to reach out across the world.

There has never been a better time to speak up for people and animals and to join others campaigning for a better, fairer world.

Why Are People Cruel?

The Psychology of animal abuse

Many children today are being raised as vegetarians and vegans and it is relatively simple for their parents to explain the issues to them in such a way that they understand why they are not being given 'cruel' things to eat.

However the main thing that such children have difficulty understanding is why 'nice' people such as their uncles and aunties and school friends do 'nasty' things such as eating and wearing dead animals. It is useful for all of us to take time every so often to think about this issue.

Some people seem to take sadistic pleasure from cruelty, but these are in the minority. We believe that most people are cruel through ignorance, or they are so detached from their fellow creatures that they are actually unable to comprehend the suffering which they are causing and to act on this. We feel that it is over-simplistic to simply dismiss people as heartless animal abusers.

We all need to accept that people who are kind and responsible in many areas of their life are also capable of contributing to cruelty. Once we feel comfortable accepting this, we should consider why this is happening. We will then be in a much stronger position to actually do something about it.

Most of the things we do and the attitudes we have towards others are based on the belief patterns which we have in our minds. These act as moral codes, or lists of 'do's' and 'don'ts' which we follow as we live our lives. We begin to form these belief patterns in our early childhood and then we adapt and add to them throughout our lives.

They are influenced by our parents, friends, peer-group, subconscious memories from lessons learned in past lives (if you believe in re-incarnation), religious teachings of your church, if applicable, and the media. Many people call the process of forming these belief systems 'socialisation'.

In Britain it is considered perfectly normal to cook and eat parts of cows and chickens, yet outrageous and abnormal to eat dog or budgerigar meat. In many parts of India, it is considered completely unacceptable to eat cows. In some countries, dogs and cats are eaten regularly and the British attitude towards these animals would be considered very strange. These are examples of speciesism, i.e. actively discriminating between different species of animal.

You could say that people are socialised to have differing attitudes to species of animals according to the historical period and culture that they grow up into.

However animal cruelty is not simply a matter of speciesism. It is more complicated than this. It is also possible for people with pet rabbits to sit down and eat a meal of rabbit, or for a vivisector who experiments on dogs for a living to form a loving relationship with a pet dog in their own home. Why is it that people are able to have such an inconsistent attitude?

A few years ago, two pigs escaped from a slaughterhouse and were on the run for several days. There was a lot of media interest in this story, in fact the pigs were named 'Butch' and 'Sundance' by the press. Once the pigs had been caught, public pressure was so strong that instead of being slaughtered, they were taken to an animal sanctuary.

No doubt some of the millions of people who followed this story stopped eating meat as a result, but the vast majority of people continued to eat as many pigs and other animals afterwards as they did before, despite the fact that they had felt genuinely relieved that these two animals were spared.

Could it be that people were able to sympathise with Butch and Sundance because they were given names? Suddenly they were no longer simply animals of the species 'pig'. They were individuals, with an identity all of their own.

Do you think that if all packaged meat products contained pictures of the animals who had died to make the product, along with a name for each animal and a brief description of his or her character, that a large proportion of people would be put off from buying the product? We think so.

What if household products which have been tested on animals were required by law to display a picture of the animals they use in their tests, showing the conditions the animals live in and the types of experiments done to them?

We think that there would be a stampede to the cruelty-free products and that market forces would soon put the vivisectors out of business!

The widespread acceptance of speciesism in our society is part of the reason why animal cruelty is still so commonplace, but it is not the only reason. We need to understand the mental process by which people can sympathise and relate to some individuals but distance themselves from others and regard their needs and feelings as irrelevant or non-existent.

If a person announces to their friends and family that they are going to stop eating meat and other animal products, consider the social pressures that will be put on that person to change their mind and discard their new-found beliefs in favour of the status quo.

Will they be called a 'wimp' by male friends? Will anxious relatives try to convince them that their health will suffer? Will they be accused of anthropomorphism? Ignorance? Rejection of their culture? Will they be called a 'spoilsport' or accused of awkwardness?

We all need to regularly examine the social pressures which cause people to do cruel things and to resist change. Once we understand this socialisation process more clearly, we are in a stronger position to fight it!

We are all a part of history. How much we help to change the course of history is up to us to decide.

Animal rights campaigning is a battle for the hearts and minds of people.

We need to challenge many of the strongest yet most subtle ideologies which influence people's behaviour.

This is not an easy task and you should not expect amazing overnight victories, but slowly the humane message is getting through and you can help it to gather pace!

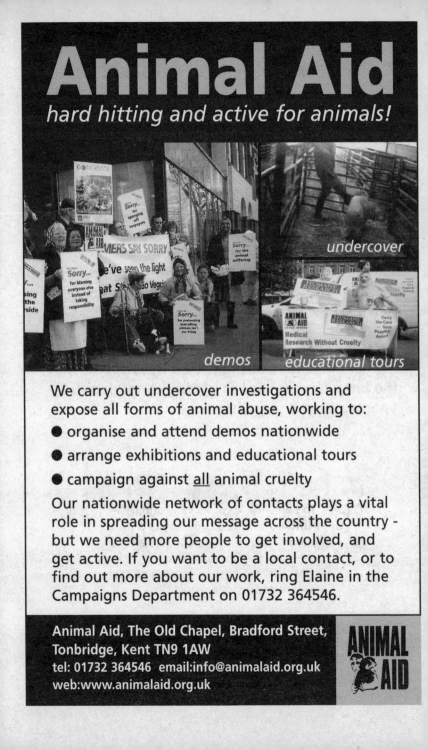

SOME INSPIRING QUOTES...

Not to hurt our humble brethren is our first duty to them, but to stop there is not enough. We have a higher mission - to be of service to them whenever they require it.

- St Francis of Assissi

All beings tremble before violence.
All fear death. All love life.
See yourself in others.
Then whom can you hurt? What harm can you do?

- Buddha, 563-483 B.C.

To be a vegetarian is to disagree - to disagree with the course of things today. Starvation, world hunger, cruelty, waste, wars, we must make a statement against these things.
Vegetarianism is my statement, and I think it is a strong one.

- Isaac Bashevis Singer

To **look** is one thing.
To **see** what you look at is another.
To **understand** what you see is a third.
To **learn** from what you understand is
still something else.
But to **act** on what you learn is all that
really matters isn't it?

- Harvard Business Review

chapter one

ANIMAL RIGHTS BEGINS ON YOUR PLATE !

"Thou shalt not kill." - God

If you still eat meat...

Perhaps you love animals and whilst you believe that you can eat animals that are slaughtered humanely, vivisection and veal are vile.

We've got news for you. Every animal farm is a concentration camp. Babies and mothers are separated, unwanted males are exterminated, worn out breeding animals are killed at a quarter of their natural life span, even on so called 'free range' or organic farms. As for humane slaughter, it's no better than saying "we have built a better gas chamber". If you doubt us, we recommend a visit to your local slaughterhouse.

Is it right to have one rule for dogs but another for equally intelligent pigs? Is it right to condemn the veal trade but munch on the calf's mother who cried and fretted for days after he was taken away to be put in a crate or turned into pet food? Is it right to haul sensitive fish out of water and leave them to slowly suffocate?

There is no such thing as cruelty free meat. The only blood-free burger is a veggie burger. The only cruelty-free sausage is a soya sausage. The only ethical fishcake is a 'fishless fishcake'!

Living without cruelty does not mean living without. Investigate

Cheatin' chicken, ham and *garlic sausage.* Choose *'Rashers'*, tempeh and *'sizzles'*. There are lots more delicious dishes that don't involve killing and cruelty. Why not invest in a cookbook and get experimenting with veggie versions of traditional meals or the delicious dishes in Asian, Indian, Middle Eastern or Thai cuisine. If you loathe cooking altogether, load up with fab fast foods at any health food shop or supermarket.

It's crazy to campaign for some animals and gorge on others. Surely they all have the right to live free, fulfilled lives. There are no nutrients in meat that aren't found in plant based foods without all the added saturated fat, cholesterol, pesticide and hormone residues, salmonella, listeria, BSE and a long list of other horrors.

There is no nutrient deficiency that is more common in vegans and veggies than meat eaters, but all degenerative diseases, such as cancer of the colon and heart disease are more common in meat eaters.

There are no convincing arguments for eating meat, but zillions against. Chuck out the chicken, bin the beef, trash the turkey and finish with fish. Your body will thank you for it with a healthier heart, more energy and on average, six extra years of life. As for the animals, they'd certainly thank you if they could.

Does Animal Abuse
Get Your Goat?

Help us **do something** about it.

Contact PETA to join our activist network.

PeTA PO Box 3169, London SW18 4WJ, England • 020 8870 3966
info@petaeurope.co.uk • PETAEurope.org

Photograph: Chip Simons

If you're a veg-eat-dairy-an...

Do you think that milk and cheese are suitable for a vegetarian diet because nothing died to make them? Think again! Mammals only produce milk after the birth of their young.

By making them pregnant every year (usually by artificial insemination) and then taking their babies away at a few days old, we are able to steal their milk. Without the dairy industry, there would be no beef and veal industries. Therefore, milk is no more acceptable to ethical vegetarians than veal.

"Hold on!" you may think, "I've just gone vegetarian and now you're suggesting that I give up cheese, too?" True, by not eating dead animals you are doing a lot more than meat eaters to help animals, so well done. It's great that you're veggie, but don't hang around there too long.

As a vegan you'll have three chances a day to save twice as many animals and sever all links with the slaughterhouse.

Maybe you have tried soya milk and didn't like it. There are several brands on the market and the strength and sweetness varies between brands. Opt for a sweetened type for a few weeks and then you'll find that cow's milk tastes disgusting and fatty. Check out your local wholefood store for vegan cheese, cream, mayonnaise, yoghurts, egg replacers and soya ice creams like *Swedish Glace, Provamel* and *Tofutti*. Examine margarine ingredients for lurking lactose, casein, whey, fish oil and other nasties.

As for eggs, 90% of them are laid by hens imprisoned in battery cages. There is no legal definition of "free range" and most so called free range hens are still kept in very cramped conditions.

A very small number of hens are allowed enough space to

exercise properly and live anything like a fulfilled life.

Remember as well that in any commercial egg farm, the male chicks are gassed or crushed to death while still only hours old, even in so called "free range", and what happens to the hens when they stop laying an egg every day or two?

Check the Resources chapter 16 for details of recommended literature and groups who can advise you on vegan products. We have also provided a list of helpful websites. We're sure that rather than missing hen's periods and cow juice, you'll wonder how you ever survived without all the hundreds of scrummy vegan delicacies just waiting to be discovered.

...we're not just talking about food.

We don't eat the inside and we won't wear the outside. You won't be taken seriously if you campaign against fur but still wear leather, which is just cow fur with the hairs scraped off, or suede, which is pig fur with the hairs scraped off, or wool which is sheep fur, because it is wrong to assume that the sheep don't mind having it removed.

Shearing is a violent process, in which the timid sheep are thrown on their backs and are usually left with cuts and bruises. 80% of wool comes from Australia, a hot country where 1/3 of sheep die from heat exhaustion and dehydration.

As with dairy cows, sheep are slaughtered at a relatively young age when their wool is losing quality. Wool and mutton, leather and beef, they're all the same bloody animal slave industry.

The modern alternatives, such as vegetarian shoes made from stuff called lorica or clothing made from goretex, thinsulate or fleece fabrics can be superior to leather and wool anyway.

The first step to becoming an activist and campaigning against animal cruelty is putting your own house in order. It's not a case of giving up things, but replacing them with better, kinder alternatives.

It's a lot easier than you might think. You can give your animal skins a decent burial, or give them away. If you can't afford to buy replacements, wear them until they fall apart and then buy something kinder next time.

The sooner you get some cruelty-free clothes, the more embarrassment you'll be spared when cocky meat-heads accuse you of hypocrisy.

If you're already vegan...

Brilliant! but don't keep it to yourself. The fact that you have picked up this book and read this far proves that you care about animal suffering and genuinely want to help stop it.

The number of animals hunted, trapped, abused in circuses and tortured in experiments each year runs into many millions, but it's small compared to the billions of animals who suffer and die as a result of animal farming. Turning vegan and encouraging other people to do so is the best way to save thousands of animals from suffering and slaughter.

VEG-EAT-DAIRY-AN

minus

EAT-DAIRY (and eggs)

=

VEG-AN !!

chapter two

SETTING UP A LOCAL GROUP

While running stalls at fairs and festivals and also on the streets, we are often approached by people who want to be put in touch with their local campaigning animal rights group.

We firmly believe that the most effective way to spread the message about animal cruelty is through the work of local activists, so we encourage the enquirer to get involved with their nearest group and look up the address for them in the *Animals Contacts Directory* which is a directory of all the local and national animal rights groups in Britain (and which also contains lots of other useful addresses, see the Resources chapter for details.)

Unfortunately, in many areas there is no local group or the group that exists is not very active. It would be wonderful if there was an active, dedicated group based in every school, college, village, town and city. If that was the case, imagine how widely information could be spread!

The idea of setting up a local campaigning group sounds daunting, but it's actually very straightforward. This chapter provides some useful hints and guidelines in order to inspire and encourage you.

CONTACTING OTHERS

The first stage in setting up a local group is to get in touch with other like-minded people in your area. One good way to do this is to place cards or posters which state your address or phone number and the fact that you want to set up a group in local shops.

We would start off with Health Food, Animal Welfare charity and general Grocers shops. Don't forget libraries.

If writing your advert on a card, keep it very brief and to the point. Make sure that important words like "animal suffering" are highlighted in some way so as to make them more eye-catching.

If shoppers are scanning through a noticeboard or window full of cards and posters you have to make sure that yours stands out from the rest and is seen by as many people as possible. Some shops make a small charge for displaying notices, others will do it free.

You can also try writing in to the letters page in your local paper. It is surprising how many people read them. You can go into much more detail in a letter and I would suggest describing some of the things that concern you, then appealing for people who feel the same way as you to get in touch. Here is an example of the sort of letter I would write:

Dear Editor,

Your recent story about the large increase in the number of people who take animal testing into consideration before buying household products and cosmetics was of interest to me. Public concern about the cruelty involved in animal experiments is growing all the time as more and more people are choosing cruelty-free goods. Awareness is also growing about bloodsports, animal circuses and the horrors of factory farming.

It is easy for those of us who care to do something to help animals. As well as not buying animal-tested products, we can avoid animal circuses and replace the animal products like meat and eggs in our diet with humane alternatives. We can also spread information locally about animal issues. I'd really like to form a group with others who care so that we can

*work together and do this. If you are interested, phone me
soon on 01234 567 89 and we'll arrange a meeting. Together
we can speak up for the animals!*

Yours sincerely,

Your Name.

Another way to contact like-minded people is to get in touch
with organisations such as environmental and human rights
groups. A lot of the people who support such causes are also
sympathetic to animal rights and vice versa. You could go
along to one of their meetings and talk to them about it or
pass around some leaflets.

Finally, while you are investigating all the other methods of
communication, don't forget about word of mouth. Mention
your plans to friends, relatives and colleagues. If they aren't
interested, they might know someone who is.

CALLING A MEETING

Once interested people have started to contact you, the next
stage is to call a meeting. This should be arranged on a date
perhaps about a month in the future, in order to give people a
chance to plan for it and to let others know. Early weekday
evenings or Sunday afternoons suit most people.

You will have to decide on a venue for the meeting. There are
advantages and disadvantages to holding it in someone's
house. The advantages are that it's free, you don't have the
hassle of booking it and you can prepare refreshments easily.

The disadvantages are that some people (especially young
people), feel awkward and intimidated about the idea of going
to a complete stranger's house, your house might not be in a
well known and accessible location, you probably won't have

enough room or chairs to accommodate an unexpectedly large turnout and unless you live alone, there are bound to be lots of distractions.

From personal experience, we would strongly recommend hiring a cheap room in a central location on main bus routes which has the facilities for you to make hot drinks. Community centres, church halls and town halls are worth trying. You might even be able to hire a room for free.

RUNNING YOUR FIRST MEETING

Before the meeting, have a good think about all the things you need to know in order to establish the group. Make a list of these things so that you can refer to it on the day. For a start, you will have to establish:

* **What the main concerns of your group will be.** Will you concentrate on campaigns against animal experiments, bloodsports, or all areas of animal abuse?

* **What type of campaigning you will do.** Will you just arrange regular street stalls and leafletting sessions or will you also run campaigns and hold demonstrations, etc. Will you produce a regular newsletter?

* **What skills and resources you have as a group.** Are there any artists or confident speakers in the group? Have any of you been in a campaigning group before? Do any of you have contacts with the press or council? Does anyone have easy access to a computer or photocopier? What about vehicles?

On the day, you should chair the meeting because you organised it. Introduce yourself by stating your name and then a brief description about why you feel concerned about animal cruelty and why you want to be in a local campaigning group, then go around the room with everyone doing the same. This

will help everyone relax and put them in the mood to talk. Read out your list of discussion points and ask if anyone else can think of something you've missed. Then draw up an agenda by putting everything into a logical order, or pass it around for everyone to add to it. Spend the rest of the meeting going through the agenda and make sure that someone who writes quickly and has clear handwriting is taking notes.

During the meeting you will all get a realistic idea about what sort of things you can organise and achieve as a group. A group is more organised and efficient if it appoints a secretary and treasurer. If one person has taken on the responsibility to deal with all the group's correspondence, it is more likely that enquiry letters etc. will be dealt with quickly and confusion about whose turn it is to deal with the mail will be avoided.

Likewise, if one person keeps up to date with the group's finances, it is easier for your group to keep in touch with how much money it is spending and to plan ahead. You might also choose to appoint a press officer, but this isn't as important and depending on how the people at the meeting feel, it could work out easier if you take it in turns to deal with the press.

At the end of the meeting you will all need to agree on a name for your group. This should reflect your principles and sound positive. A short name or one with initials which spell a word (an acronym) is easier to remember.

You will also need to agree on a contact address and/or phone number. From personal experience we suggest that you set up a PO Box. Enquire about this at any main Post Office.

If you are going to be promoting your group widely it is not a good idea to use someone's private address. The phone number should be that of someone who intends to be active within the group who is in a lot of the time or who has an

answering machine.
You will also need to sort out when and where your next
meeting will be held. If you establish a time which you will
stick to, for example 7pm on the first Tuesday of each month,
you can all make a note of this and future confusion will be
avoided.

Finally, we suggest compiling a telephone list so that you can
all keep in touch with each other, or at least make sure that
the secretary makes a note of everyone's phone numbers.
There will be times when people have to be contacted in a
hurry or things have to be discussed with everyone but there
isn't time to call a meeting.

After the meeting, the secretary should write up a report about
what was discussed and what decisions were made and then
circulate this to everyone before the second meeting. If
everyone present agrees to pay a small subscription fee, this
will cover photocopying and postage costs. Your group may
decide to introduce a membership fee at some point in the
future.

SUMMARY

1. Get in touch with other like-minded people by advertising
the fact that you want to set up a group.

2. Organise a meeting at a suitable venue and make a list of
important things to discuss and questions to ask everyone.

3. Find out what skills, resources and contacts your group
has.

4. Decide what kind of activities the group is going to get
involved in and what issues it will campaign about.

5. Appoint a secretary and treasurer and decide what
responsibilities those people will have.

6. Decide on a contact address and 'phone number.

7. Choose a name for the group which reflects its aims and principles.

8. Decide on the time, date and venue for your next meeting.

9. Make sure that the secretary takes a note of everyone's address and 'phone number and also compiles and circulates a report of what was decided at the meeting.

10. Set up your own website.

11. Have fun, make friends and focus your ideas.

Stop Huntingdon Animal Cruelty

Huntingdon Life Sciences own three laboratories where they torture animals. At their largest site in Cambridgeshire they kill 500 animals everyday. They have been exposed five times revealing severe animal cruelty.

Stop Huntingdon Animal Cruelty aim to close down HLS. If you want to help the animals suffering inside their labs please contact us at the address shown below.

This beagle suffered and died inside HLS.

Stop Huntingdon Animal Cruelty, PO Box 381, Cheltenham, Glos, GL50 1YN. Tel: 0121 632 6460 Web: www.shac.net Email: info@shac.u-net.com

chapter three

INITIATING AND RUNNING A LOCAL CAMPAIGN

The most important role of local animal rights groups and contacts over the years has been to set up and run campaigns in their area.

This is not nearly as daunting as it sounds. Some groups choose one local campaign and concentrate almost entirely on that alone, diverting almost all of the group's time and resources into the one campaign.

It makes more sense however to have two or three campaigns running at the same time, as different campaigns require different approaches and strategies and the views and priorities of group members will differ. This approach is also more likely to attract new members into your group, as your group will come across as more dynamic and active.

Examples of typical campaigns:
1. Getting a local establishment closed down, such as a fur shop or zoo.
2. Getting something banned, such as the sale of cats and dogs in pet shops, angling in a park or circuses on council land.
3. Promoting cruelty free living in your area, such as persuading food retailers to sell more vegan meals and snacks or producing a guide to ethical eating and shopping locally.
4. Joining in with a national campaign, such as live exports or stopping culling of badgers by the Ministry of Agriculture.
5. Protest marches.

When you've formulated your plan, it's time to act.

Success depends on dreaming, thinking, planning and then action.

The rest of this chapter will examine each type of campaign in turn. The best way to do this is to use a fictitious group, 'Anytown Animal Action', as an example.

1. GETTING A LOCAL ESTABLISHMENT CLOSED

The Zoo

At one of their meetings, AAA decide that they don't like the idea that the local zoo is making money from exploiting animals and they wish they could stop it from doing so. They are aware that the zoo is very small and that it has a mixture of 'domestic' and wild animals on display.

They are concerned that some of the larger animals might be in enclosures which are far too small for them and they are also worried about the effect on the animals of a fairground which is right next door to the zoo.

The more they discuss it, the more they realise that they really want to do something about the welfare of the zoo animals. They decide to try to close the zoo down by producing a leaflet which exposes the cruel conditions in Anytown Zoo and which questions the existence of zoos as a whole.

The group decide to hold regular demonstrations at the entrance to the zoo at which they will hand out the leaflet, display posters and banners and talk to the people going into the zoo. They hope to change enough people's minds about going into the zoo that it will make much less money from entrance fees and be forced to close. They will also publicise the issue as much as possible in the local media, make themselves available to give talks in local schools and hold a public meeting.

This approach ensures that every possible technique of communication is used to get your message out there and also that all the members of the group can get involved because everybody's skills can be utilised effectively. For example, some people are brilliant at doing media interviews, but would panic at the thought of standing in front of a room full of schoolchildren, whilst others are computer wizards who know how to effortlessly produce dramatic posters and newsletters but would prefer to keep a low profile and avoid any contact with crowds.

Now that they have decided what they are going to do, they start gathering the information they need. In order to write a leaflet which is accurate and contains enough detail to be convincing and in order to get photographs to use on their leaflet and in their displays, the group decide that one of them will have to go into the zoo with a camera and notebook. One of them does this, reluctantly paying their entrance fee because they know that it's worth giving the zoo a little bit of money now in order to stop them making lots of money in the near future.

Another member contacts all the national animal welfare organisations which concentrate on zoos, and asks them whether they have any specific information on this particular zoo which would be of help in the campaign.

In any campaign, it is absolutely essential to research your target thoroughly. This will ensure that you have all the information that you need to present your case to the public. You simply cannot afford to make embarrassing mistakes which could cost your group vital credibility if your opponents or the local press pick up on your blunders.

The group hold a special meeting at which they read through all the notes and look at the photographs that were collected by the member who visited the zoo. They decide what they want to include in the leaflet and some artistic members of the group start work on placards with anti-zoo slogans and display boards containing information and photographs.

A member with a computer offers to type up the leaflet and another member takes responsibility for getting it printed, shopping around locally for the best deal as printing and photocopying costs vary so widely.

The group choose a date for their first protest. They decide to hold it on a Sunday because this is the day the zoo gets the most visitors. A few days before the demonstration, press releases are faxed out to the local papers by the person acting as press officer.

After the first demonstration, the group meet up again to discuss tactics. They decide how regularly to hold their protests and set about organising a public meeting. They begin stepping up the campaign gradually, monitering the local press and networking with groups in other areas who have run similar campaigns in the past.

How to Close Down a Fur Shop

Aim to picket outside every day during the peak fur-selling season, i.e. Autumn and Winter (if possible!) until the shop shuts. If your group only has a handful of members, this won't be possible, so concentrate on the peak hours of 1-3pm and Saturdays. Have at least two people at each door of the shop with a petition, and a couple of boards showing the real truth behind the fur trade. Offer a leaflet to anyone walking past. If you can't make it every day, identify the key days when the shop gets the most customers.

Don't verbally abuse people going in as this gives the law an excuse to move you. If you shout things like, "You heartless scummy bitch, how can you be so cruel?", the police can interpret this as harrassment and you may be cautioned or arrested. If, however, you shout "The fur trade is an evil trade, don't support cruelty", you are not directly insulting anyone or causing them distress and harassment.

Your presence outside the shop is enough to deter most people from going in. You must keep it up. It will take weeks or months, not days, to close the place down but it's a fantastic motivator for your group when the place shuts.

Several local groups have had repeated successes with this tactic. Different police officers interpret the lawfulness of these tactics in different ways. If they threaten to arrest you, it's up to you whether you wish to go along with that and stand your ground. After all, you have a right to peacefully protest and if charges are brought against you, they are unlikely to stand up in court.

Within the last few years, some fur shop owners have been fighting back against groups who target their shops by using their solicitors to issue an injunction against named groups or individuals which stops them from demonstrating in a named area (usually the whole of, or part of the street in which the shop is located). This is enforceable by police and they can arrest you simply for breaching the injunction.

As a result of this, campaigners have had to revise their tactics and apply pressure on such retailers in more subtle ways.

It is best to avoid calling each other by surname within earshot of the shopkeeper. Try not to let them take your photograph for the same reason. Don't let them intimidate you - they may try to, because after all, you are trying to put them out of business and they are unlikely to passively accept this. If possible, always have a dictaphone, video camera or recording Walkman to record whatever the staff say to you when they come out, as this may be very important if you have to later deal with the law.

Groups have been known to list the names and addresses of the owners and directors of fur shops on leaflets and in newsletters in order to encourage people to contact them with enquiries. This information is available to the public through Companies House.

Campaigners should ensure that they are fully aware of the correct wording on the injunction and exactly whom the named people on it are, so it is best to advise all of the members of your group to ask the solicitors acting on behalf of the shop to send them a copy of the injunction. Doing so will also cost the shop a considerable amount of money, as solicitors will charge them for every letter that they send.

Happily though, these injunctions do not stop the protests being effective, as several fur shops who used them have gone out of business in recent years.

If you want further advice about this tactic, contact Fur Free London, BM2248, London, WC1N 3XX.

2. GETTING SOMETHING BANNED

This is a speciality of local groups. Keep an eye out for disgusting practices taking place in your area and try to get them banned.

For example, AAA found out that foxes were being shot on a local golf course. They looked into this in order to establish who was doing the shooting, when it was happening, how many foxes were being killed and what the reasoning behind this was.

Armed with this information, they produced a leaflet and petition about this subject and then organised a demonstration at the course, contacting the local media.

They then organised a public meeting in order to raise even more awareness about this subject. They launched a letter writing campaign, flyposters etc. and kept up the pressure until they had embarrassed the course owners into submission!

3. PROMOTING ETHICAL LIVING LOCALLY

You can produce an **information booklet** which describes the best places to get vegetarian and vegan food in your area and also provides advice and encouragement for prospective vegans. Some veggie-friendly pubs and cafes might be happy to display your posters and leaflets if they know that you are promoting them to your members and friends.

Why not produce a **street map** with recommended shops and cafes clearly marked? List anywhere that provides a good service for vegetarians and vegans. Give a summary of the opening hours, prices and type of food offered.

We recommend including some omnivorous establishments as well as the totally veggie ones, because this will encourage them to recognise their veggie customers as more important and they are more likely to offer new vegan dishes if they have new customers coming in asking them to.

You could perhaps organise and publicise a **guided tour** of your town for the benefit of both veggie newcomers to your area and local people just turning veggie. You can also promote cruelty free household products, etc.

If you would like more information about how to do this, contact **Vegetarian Guides** (info@vegetarianguides.com or write to the address on page 4).

4. JOINING IN WITH A NATIONAL CAMPAIGN

Many of the national societies run campaigns such as
National Vegetarian Week, World Day of action against
McDonalds and World Vegan Day. You can organise and run
publicity stunts along these themes. Use your imagination.....

PICKETING McDONALD'S (or similar burger outlets)

You can do a **litter dump**. Collect all the cartons and cups
strewn around the streets near McDonalds and take it back -
this is perfectly legal and will grab the attention of all the
customers and possibly make them feel rightly ashamed. Be
prepared for hassle from their security guards or more mouthy
members of staff if you do this.

You can also do a sit-in where lots of you go in, sit down, take
out your own food and start eating it. When the police arrive,
you just leave. Of course, you can use their clean, free toilets
any time!

Many campaigners dislike using such tactics, however as they
feel that it simply alienates you from the public and makes you
look like you are just out to cause trouble. Do think things
through with your group as there are pros and cons to any
tactic.

With a licence from the Council, you can set up a **free veggie
burger stall** in the middle of town and give them away with
anti-McDonald's literature. You will need to borrow a small
catering trailer in order to do this. You'll take more in
donations than the cost of the food. This is a very positive
kind of demonstration. You can get all the literature and
advice on this tactic from Veggies Catering Campaign.

Another tactic has been developed very recently which is
even more easy to organise. Buy or borrow some freezer
boxes or bags, the sort of carry-case people use to transport
food in an insulated environment. Line the insides and lids of

these with a couple of layers of silver foil.

Cook a load of veggie burgers in the normal way and prepare a corresponding number of salad rolls, by slicing bread rolls in half, filling with salad (for example, a slice of tomato, a slice of cucumber and a bit of lettuce) and perhaps a bit of relish. Wrap the outside in kitchen roll to minimise any contact with your fingers.

Next, soak some towels in water and microwave them for a minute or so until they are steaming hot, or boil them in water if you don't have a microwave. Put them into carrier bags and line some of the freezer boxes with them. Carefully fill these boxes with the cooked burgers. They should stay hot for several hours. Fill more boxes or bags with the salad rolls. If it is a hot day, place an ice pack in the bottom of these containers.

Each person can carry a box or bag in each hand and you can effortlessly travel into a city centre and start to hand the burgers out. A pair of tongs are essential for enabling you to quickly pick hot burgers from the hot box and slot them into the salad rolls from the cold box.

You should either have impressive visual display boards or keep shouting out 'free veggie burgers!'

Make sure you hand each customer a leaflet, so that they know exactly what point you are trying to make. This tactic is easy, legal and prevents any wastage, as any unused burgers can be frozen and eaten by your group.

It is vital to ensure good hygiene practices are followed if you intend to do this. Tie your hair back when preparing and serving food as stray hairs can find their way into veggie burgers very easily. You might be able to study a basic food hygiene course either very cheaply or free in your local area, ask some adult education colleges or your job centre.

5. PROTEST MARCHES

These can range from awe-inspiring, spectacular events where thousands of people bring a town centre to a temporary standstill and the streets echo with chanting, to badly organised, embarrassing flops where a dozen people half-heartedly walk about feeling self-conscious and attracting puzzled stares from passers by. Ensure that your march resembles the former type. This requires plenty of advance planning.

A protest march can only go ahead with the permission of the police. A confident and respectable-looking person in your group should approach them in order to sort out the date and route.

Study a street map of the town before meeting them and choose two or three possible routes, aiming to get maximum visibility. Try to avoid routes that go down back streets, and be ready at the meeting for the police to be awkward and try to steer you away from the main part of town where people will see you.

Find somewhere to finish, preferably where shoppers will come and listen, such as a town square, or failing that a field or other open space where stalls can be put up. Get permission from the owners of the space to gather there at the end and to put up stalls. If it's a public place you will need a licence from the Licensing Department of the Council.

The police will demand that they have only one person to liaise with up to the march and on the day of it. They will understand that you won't be able to give them a very accurate prediction of the expected turnout, so they won't regard it as a major problem if more people come than expected.

The police will also insist on one steward for every 50

expected demonstrators, who should ensure the safety of the marchers. They must wear something that distinguishes them such as a fluorescent bib or armband. You can just buy some material and wrap it round arms, or get flashy armbands on loan from some of the national groups.

Allow plenty of time to promote your march, at least 2 months, preferably about 6! Advertise wherever possible, in animal rights magazines, local papers, local radio, local TV. Press release the march details two weeks in advance to all local media. Press release again to everyone two days before the march. You can also promote your event in any local *'What's On'* listings. See if the national press will mention your event as well. (There's no harm in trying!) Contact national animal welfare and 'green' type publications as well, even low circulation ones.

If you get permission for stalls, invite other local charitable organizations to have one. Why not organise caterers as well.

Don't make the march more than 2 or 3 miles and check the route to ensure there are no road closures. Make sure that the route doesn't present problems to young children or disabled people.

Hire or scrounge public address equipment for the end of the march and arrange speakers. Make sure they keep to a short time (no more than 5 minutes per speaker) and forbid waffle.

Make it media friendly with plenty to photograph. Depending on the subject, make sure you have children or animal costumes at the front, a wooden crate for a veal calf demo, or cages, banners and home-made placards. You could even have people dressed as grim reapers or crazy experimenters with blood-splattered laboratory coats!

You can make a **banner** from a big sheet. Design it on paper, then draw it onto the sheet with a pencil, then paint it with gloss paint or any paint that won't wash off. You can make a really eye-catching banner by sewing on letters in bright material. If you're going to march with your banner then cut holes, for example in the O's, to let the wind through or you'll get blown all over the place.

To make **placards**, get some light plastic from a D.I.Y store. It can be corrugated. Cut to A3 or A2 size and stick a poster on it. Smaller colour posters can be blown up to A3 size in a colour photocopy shop, or in two pieces to A2. Cover the poster with sticky-backed plastic. Then nail the plastic board through the middle to a stick of light wood. You can nail one on each side. Now you have a long-lasting placard.

For a big march, make up about forty of these, though a handful would be adequate for the front line which is what you want photographed for the media. The more the better though. If you are in a hurry and want to knock together a large number of placards, just use cardboard and don't bother with the sticky plastic. Just be sure the words are clear and can be seen from a distance.

A protest march must be noisy. Ensure that someone has a loudhailer and that whistles are handed out. Drums work well as when beaten slowly they encourage everybody to walk more slowly and when beaten quickly, they can whip a crowd up into a frenzy.

These are just a few suggestions. Demos can range from two people giving out leaflets to a huge protest march. Just use your imagination and tailor your demo according to the target, expected turnout and likely response from the public and press.

Remember, the most effective stunt is the one that's never been done before!

Some Success Stories

Consort beagle breeders, Hillgrove Farm cat breeders, Regal Rabbits and Shamrock Farm monkeys were all places which supplied animals for experiments.

All these places have closed down in recent years, as a direct result of concentrated, full-time national campaigns being run against them by animal rights groups.

What these groups did was to fund-raise for months in order to raise thousands of pounds, whilst researching their target thoroughly.

They then got glossy, full colour leaflets, posters and a newsletter printed and launched their campaign by distributing these as widely as they could. The newsletter and posters gave details of their first national demonstration.

An effective tactic has been to produce two types of poster; a 'cute' one showing an attractive picture of some animals and a 'gory' one, showing a shocking scene of cruelty. This is because some people do not respond to shock tactics, they just turn away. Also, some places such as shops and libraries will not display unpleasant images, but will happily put up a poster showing a rabbit or kitten.

What these groups realised is that if you want large numbers of people to come along to your events and you want them to circulate your posters and leaflets, you have to have glossy and professional-looking literature. This costs a lot more than simple black and white printing, but if you are serious about mounting a national campaign on this scale, it is the way you have to go.

These groups made sure that their targets were hit from all angles. Their newsletters included names and addresses of directors of the company and also of companies which supplied goods and services to the target company, so that pressure could be put on them as well.

Companies with shares were also listed and pressure was put on them to sell the shares. If they showed no sign of doing so, demonstrations were organised.

Websites were set up, with up-to-the-minute information about what was happening with the campaign.

We believe that the Hillgrove campaign took about 18 months to close down their target. The Regal Rabbits campaign took 6 days!!!

At the time of going to print, the Save the Newchurch Guinea Pigs and Stop Huntingdon Animal Cruelty campaigns are still going strong. They have achieved a lot, but could really do with some more help. Their addresses are included in the Resources chapter.

chapter four

PRODUCING LEAFLETS AND POSTERS

The most important part of campaigning is spreading information and one very effective way to do this is through the distribution of leaflets.

Many of the groups listed in the Resources section will supply a variety of leaflets free or cheaply priced, but if you want to promote your group and its activities or you run a local campaign against a particular establishment, you will need to produce your own. In order to put the message across effectively, your leaflets need to be eye-catching and readable. This chapter advises how to produce such leaflets on a low budget and we have provided some examples.

EFFECTIVE WORDING

In order to put your message across effectively, you need to make sure that your leaflet is concise, but that it contains enough information to win the public over to your argument.

Several of you should have a brainstorming session in which you list all the important points which your leaflet will cover. Imagine that one of you is a curious member of the public who feels concerned about animals but really hasn't got a clue why anyone should want to protest against the trade or establishment in question.

Just write down anything which comes into your head, as in the following example of a campaign against a small zoo.

Anytown Zoo

What types of animals does the zoo have?
What conditions are they kept in?
Give some examples of animals which are kept in particularly cruel conditions and the effects these conditions are having on their mental and physical health.
Deal with the 'conservation' argument.
Point out that zoos are not educational for children.
Appeal to people not to visit the zoo.
Explain what will happen to the animals if the zoo closes.
Explain what else people can do to help stop the cruelty.

Then turn what you have written into a brief 'essay', which makes it clear why your group strongly objects to the zoo and wants it to close and that such zoos only exist because people pay their admission to go in.

AGREED WORDING FOR ZOO LEAFLET

Animal Welfare

Thousands of animals in zoos worldwide are driven mad by captivity. In the wild, animals spend much of their time searching for food, avoiding predators and interacting with each other. In zoos, animals suffer enforced idleness, deprived of their natural environment, social groups and behaviour patterns, Together with the unnatural lighting, diet, noise levels and proximity of human visitors and alien species, this leads to obsessive, repetitive behaviour, such as pacing, rocking, circling, licking, bar biting and self mutilation. At Anytown Zoo, our investigators have watched adult chimpanzees smearing their own waste on the enclosure walls and a snow leopard pacing up and down along the side of the enclosure.

Zoos insist that 'their'animals are healthy, yet the truth is that many zoo animals die from illnesses caused by the unsuitable climate, unfamiliar parasites and contact with humans and other animals. Other zoo animals are killed or injured as a result of malnutrition, eating their young, poisoning, use of drugs and anaesthetics, and fighting brought on by the stress of their cramped conditions.

Conservation

There are 4,000 species on the endangered species list, only about 100 are being bred in zoos and of these only a handful have been released back into the wild. The flaws in captive breeding programmes include the unnatural selection of mates and the difficulty of reintroducing into the wild animals mentally and physically scarred by captivity.

The vast amounts of money needed for these programmes could be far better used conserving animals AND their habitats, funding anti-poaching patrols, educating local populations about animals and encouraging less destructive farming methods.
Out of all the species displayed at Anytown Zoo, few are described as 'endangered or vulnerable'. What possible justification is there for exhibiting the others?

What You Can Do

Don't visit any zoo or safari park.
Write to Annie Malibuser, Zoo Manager, Anytown Zoo,

Princes Park, nr Pleasureland Anytown, with your view of the zoo. Complain about the continued captivity of wild animals. Write to the local authority asking for an urgent review of the licence issued to the zoo.

The group then typed this information up and laid it out as a double sided A5 leaflet using a desktop publishing programme, adding large headings and a photo, along with the address of their group.

HOW TO LAY OUT YOUR LEAFLET

There are several approaches to this. Experiment a bit and then settle on a style you feel comfortable with. We suggest that you order a selection of sample leaflets from national societies, then sit down and study them carefully.

Think about what makes these leaflets informative and eye catching and look at the way in which some text has been highlighted to make it look more important. Then take lots of scrap paper and have a go at drawing up your own.

As an example on the next page is an excellent leaflet produced by London Animal Action.

ARE YOU FED UP WITH CRUELTY TO ANIMALS?

THEN GIVE US A HAND!

If you are sickened by the many forms of animal abuse all around us - the meat trade and factory farming, fur shops and coats, animal experiments, circuses and zoos, bloodsports, unwanted pets, etc - you are not alone! There is a group of people in London who are actively campaigning against such cruelties and for an alternative way of life that is not based on the exploitation of people, animals and the environment. We are called London Animal Action.

The Group: London Animal Action was formed in 1994 to build unity amongst campaigners and is an amalgamation of three previously existing groups: London Boots Action Group, London Animal Rights Coalition and London Anti-Fur Campaign. We cover the whole of the city, act as co-ordinator for other local groups in the capital, and publish a monthly newsletter, *London Animal Rights News*. As well as campaigning against all forms of animal abuse, we hold meetings and information stalls to educate the public. We do not carry out illegal actions as a group but recognise the effectiveness of direct action. Some of our members take part in hunt sabbing and we provide support for people who have been imprisoned for animal rights activities, by writing letters, visiting prisoners and demonstrations at court appearences. We are an open group without any leaders or hierachy and welcome anyone who shares our aim of total animal liberation. For more details please turn the page.

chapter five

STREET STALLS

The main activity of most local groups is running street stalls. This is a very effective way to distribute information whilst communicating with the public and fund raising. Street stalls enable your group to give out lots of leaflets and also discuss animal issues with the public on a one to one level.

If your group regularly holds stalls in a town centre, people will get used to your presence and will remember to look out for you if they want more information on any particular subject.

HOW TO SET UP A STALL

Before your group sets up its first stall, you'll have to find out two things:

1) Where to position it.
2) Whether you need to get permission first.

The best place to put a stall is on a busy paved shopping precinct, preferably in a sheltered position. We would suggest that two or three of your group go for a walk around your nearest precinct with a notebook and draw a rough plan of the streets, marking on it any suitable looking sites. You should bear in mind that your stall must not block any shop fire exits or obstruct the pedestrian flow.

Once you have decided upon the best site for your stall, you will need to find out whether or not you need permission to have one. There is no law against setting up a stall, but each council has its own set of bye-laws regarding its highways.

Some councils will allow you to hold stalls anywhere in the precinct whenever you like, but not if you are openly collecting money.

Others have very strict restrictions and will only allow stalls in one or two places and you have to obtain a written permit first. Most fall somewhere in between.

In order to find out what type of policy your local council has, you can either contact your local town hall and enquire about this, or simply go along and set up your stall and then wait and see if the police or a council official asks you to move. If so, then they consider that you are creating an obstruction and they do have a right to move you, because obstruction of the highway is a criminal offence.

Indoor precincts are usually privately owned with their own security guards and you are unlikely to be able to get permission to set up a stall anywhere in one.

WHAT TO PUT ON THE STALL

As a group, you will need to decide on the theme for your stall. There are two distinct types of stall, the general information stall and the single issue stall.

The General Information Stall

If you want to educate the public about a wide range of different animal issues and encourage debate and discussion, you should opt for a general information stall. This should contain the following;

* A range of leaflets which cover a wide variety of subjects. We suggest having one on vivisection, one on bloodsports, one on zoos and/or circuses, one promoting the neutering and spaying of animals, one on fur, two or three on animal farming, two or three general animal rights leaflets and one

promoting your group and encouraging people to join.

* **Free or cheaply priced booklets and information sheets.**
These should contain further information about the issues in
your leaflets or vegan recipes for people to try.

* **A folder or photograph album** full of photographs which
show different examples of animal cruelty. You can cut photos
out of animal rights magazines or write off to national groups
for pictures to use. A booklet has recently been produced by
ARCnews called **Betrayed** which is full of shocking black and
white pictures.

* **Petitions**. We suggest having two petitions about different
subjects, one contentious and one very 'populist', such as
vivisection, hunting or the fur trade.

Don't have a cluttered and untidy stall, at it will turn
people away before they have even read your
leaflets. People are used to looking at immaculate
shop windows.

The Single Issue Stall

This differs from the general information stall in that you use
only one type of petition. It is best to have one with a relatively
non-contentious theme, one that the majority of people have
some degree of sympathy for, such as hunting, testing on
animals or the fur trade. You can still have a variety of leaflets,
but you concentrate on giving out the leaflets which directly
relate to the petition.

HOW TO ARRANGE A STALL

Through trial and error, we have found that the best way to
arrange a stall is as follows:

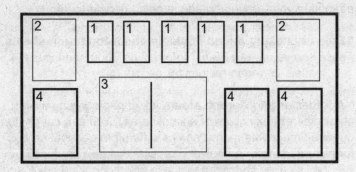

1 = leaflets
2 = pile of info booklets
3 = folder full of photographs
4 = petitions

This type of stall is useful for attracting larger numbers of people over. This means that you can distribute a larger amount of leaflets on your chosen issue and it also means that you will be offered more donations from people.

To give an example, you could run stalls which target a well known research company which tests products on animals. The display boards could show pictures of some of the experiments carried out.

When people come over, they could be asked to sign the petition and when they have finished doing so, they could be offered a leaflet which goes into more detail about the experiments carried out and what people can do to help stop them.

Often people will offer donations. It is legal to accept such donations if they are offered to you, but illegal to ask for them.

If you don't have a collecting tin or other container and there is no sign anywhere on your stall asking for money, you aren't breaking the law because nobody can claim that you are actually asking for money.

This arrangement means that people can easily reach the petitions and can clearly see the leaflets when they look up again after signing. Those people who want to read through a booklet or look through the photographs can pick them up and then stand to the side so that they don't obstruct anyone.

The piles of leaflets should be kept tidy and safe from being blown away by the wind. You can either use elastic bands or weigh them down with large stones. The petitions should be kept on clip boards and on windy days you can stop them flapping about by stretching an elastic band around the bottom.

It is up to your group which type of stall to run. Both have their advantages and disadvantages. If you feel confident enough, you can make your stalls even more effective by calling out to people to come and sign your petitions. Shout such slogans as "Help us to stop animal abuse, it only takes a moment of your time. Please sign our petition against...."

IF YOU DO STALLS REGULARLY

Always get the posters you stick on the stall laminated, to protect them from rain, wear and tear. High street copying shops like Prontaprint are expensive for this, so try back street shops and look under Laminating in the Yellow Pages. At the laminators, always go for the middle grade of plastic.

The best posters to display are either ones which show 'cute' pictures of animals which stir peoples' concience as they walk past, or gory ones which leave a lasting impression.

Different people respond to different types of visuals.

Shock tactics motivate some people, but repel others. Cute pictures really bring people over, but don't necessarily drive your message home powerfully. Most people really pay attention to bright colours or ironic humour.

Advertisers know all this and make a living out of experimenting with differing forms of visual communication. We should learn from their tactics.

chapter six

ORGANISING A PUBLIC MEETING

These are a brilliant way to raise your group's profile, attract new members, give out a lot of information and recruit support for a specific campaign. They do however require a lot of organising and even if you charge a small admission, or appeal for donations on the night, there is no guarantee that you'll recover your costs.

The first step is to call a meeting of any people in your group who are interested in helping to do the organising. The following things will need to be arranged:

> topic
> time and date
> venue
> publicity
> public address system (PA) if you are using a big hall
> speakers (people to speak, not PA!)
> catering
> funding
> videos or slides to show
> info stalls.

The group needs to decide exactly what the topic of your meeting is going to be. It should be a single issue, preferably a local one.

You then need to decide how you are going to structure the meeting.

Will you have one speaker or several? Will you show slides or videos? How long will the meeting last?

Decide which day of the week to hold your meeting. From personal experience, we recommend weekday evenings. Most people are busy Friday and Saturday nights, so these are the worst times!

The best time to start the meeting is between 7 and 8pm, which gives working people a chance to go home and get changed. If you start much later, people who are relying on public transport to get home will start leaving early. In the following example, you'll see how Anytown Animal Action organised their meeting.

The group decided to hold a meeting about the cruel conditions in their local zoo. They sat down and discussed how they were going to arrange the meeting. They invited a speaker from a national organisation that campaigns on behalf of captive animals, as well as one of their own group volunteering to give a talk. They planned to show a video and some slides that had been taken when one of the group made an 'inspection' visit to the zoo.

One of the group made enquiries and then booked a hall which was big enough to seat a hundred or so people with room left for several stalls. She deliberately chose a hall in the town centre with parking nearby so that it could be reached easily by car, bus and train. She made sure the hall was cheap and had disabled access.

Another group member booked a speaker to give an in-depth talk on the subject and he also made sure that the group had plenty of leaflets, posters etc. to stock a stall with.

Other members drew up some posters and flyers about the event, then got them printed. They then distributed them widely in the area. They did this about a month beforehand.

A rough agenda was drawn up by several of the group.

7.00pm doors open
7.10pm introductory talk by a group member, during which slides of zoo are shown.
7.30pm video
7.40pm questions from audience
8.00pm break for refreshments and time to look at stalls
8.30pm guest speaker
8.45pm summing up and appeal by group for support in their campaign
9.00pm end of meeting... more time to look at stalls, buy food etc.
9.30pm doors close. Group tidy up hall.

As well as the refreshments stall, the group arranged to have several campaigning stalls. One was a group literature stall, containing leaflets and fact sheets covering a wide variety of animal issues. Another one was for merchandise, such as posters and badges, and two were for related groups (such as the local Hunt Saboteurs and the Green Group) to use in order to promote their work.

On the day, just before the doors opened, the group had someone on the door to greet people and direct them to the right room. They ensured that the information stalls were all set up and ready and they put a leaflet about their group on each person's chair.

The group tried as hard as they could to stick to the agenda and not run overtime.

They didn't want to risk having to rush the last parts of the meeting.

SUMMARY

1. Call a special planning meeting in order to discuss theme of meeting and the important details such as date, venue etc. and who is going to take responsibility for organising what.

2. Publicise the meeting and arrange speakers, stalls, PA etc.

3. Make sure that everyone has a specific job to do on the day, eg. collecting donations, making announcements, and that they do it!

MAKING POSTERS

If you have access to a computer with desk top publishing (DTP) facilities, excellent. This is by far the easiest way to produce a poster. Failing that you'll have to use the old fashioned cut and paste method.

A poster needs to be very attention grabbing and easy to read quickly, so it can't contain too much information. When you look at advertising, for example on bus shelters, note the way they are arranged and how they've been carefully designed to attract and hold your attention and put their message across effectively. The formula is:

Attention - get it
Information - tell 'em what you're up to
Desire - make sure you've made it sound worth following up
Action - tell 'em where to go or what to do

You need a headline or title or slogan printed in BIG LETTERS which is the most eye-catching part of the whole poster. It's best to put this at the top.

Underneath put a picture or other graphic and the rest of the information which you want to get across.

A common situation where you are likely to produce a poster is when your group has organised an event and you need to publicise it. Remember the five W's: who, what, when, where and why. This is all the information your poster needs to put across. Do so in as few words as possible. The most important W's are what and when.

For example, Anytown Animal Action organised a meeting. They photocopied and circulated posters advertising the meeting. At the top was the headline: PUBLIC MEETING. Underneath: Come to our public meeting about animal rights to find out how you can help stop cruelty in Anytown. 7.30pm, Monday 5th December, Function Room, Town Hall. Free admission. Bring your friends.

They included an attractive picture of an animal. This was a simple but striking drawing, not a photo which when photocopied looks terrible from a distance.

Perhaps your group could produce a standard poster with a box at the bottom where you can fill in the details about the time and venue by hand. You can then save costs by producing a very large number of these posters at once and use them for a succession of different meetings.

Posters will stand out better if they're printed on brightly coloured paper. You will probably have to start off by photocopying rather than printing your posters because printing small batches is not cost effective. Shop around for cheap bulk photocopying in your area, for example at office superstores.

Disclaimer: Please bear in mind that if you wish to display posters in a public place you must obtain permission from the owner of the site. Otherwise you will be flyposting which the police and local council can prosecute you for.

We recommend that you have a good look around your town at the posters, fly-posters and advertisements on display there. Which ones 'jump out' at you? Which ones tell you all you need to know straight away? Which are the clearest to read and understand?

Make a mental note of the types of poster that you like and copy their layout.

(We have to do it for them...)

chapter seven

THE MEDIA

How can I get into the Press, Radio and TV?
IT'S EASY when you know how. Here's how....

A story in an animal rights or vegetarian magazine will be read by a few thousand people who are already on the side of the animals. But a story in your local paper could reach **everyone** in your area, including the many thousands who are ready to do something for animals but don't even know that your group exists to help them.

WHAT THE MEDIA WANT

The media - press, radio and tv - shapes public opinion. But they only print what they want to, or what the government and their advertisers allow. Once you know what are their criteria for using or rejecting stories, you can make sure that you feed them just the right materials to maximise your chance of reaching the public.

Picking a Media Stunt

To get a story in the local media you will need to have a local angle. Children and animals are very popular with editors. Newspapers love photos. A TV story needs to be very photogenic.

It may not be politically correct, but if your group contains someone who fits the media stereotype of cute, you may as well make use of it. So a children's protest with balloons and people in animal costumes has a good chance of making the front page, whereas a talk to adults with slides in a church hall will probably be buried.

A protest march has a great chance of being covered, particularly if you do crazy stunts like dressing up as giant vegetables, or if the subject of your protest is a controversial local issue.

Unfortunately it's also true that marches are more likely to be covered nationally if there are arrests, as we've seen with live exports protests. The national media there were initially more interested in violence and confrontation than in the animals.

If during a march a few people sit down outside the premises of a dodgy company and get arrested, there will almost certainly be a mention in the news unless a huge story breaks elsewhere, but you may not get a permit for the same demo next year.

LOCAL PRESS

Local papers are always looking for good local stories, so if you do it right it shouldn't be too hard to get coverage for some of your group's activities. **The emphasis must be on local stories or national stories with a local slant.** Make use of local supporters so you can quote a genuinely local spokesperson. Remember, local papers tend to avoid shock, horror stories. Humour always works well.

In Britain, weekly local papers are often published around Wednesday, so if you want to guarantee newspaper coverage, you'll need to send a **press release** to them about two weeks before your planned event. You can send it directly to the news editor, the editor, or better still ring up and ask if any of the journalists are vegetarian and make sure they get copies too.

Press releases all have a similar basic structure. They should be very short, enticing and contain enough information to get their interest so that they'll phone to interview you and get a story. At the top must be the title of the event or an eye-catching heading.

In the first sentence say what your event is. Follow with a brief description, no longer than two sentences, of what the event is about. Include some quotes from members of your group, for example "Fred Billings from AAA says the battery cage is the cruellest method of keeping birds...." Try to think of some punchy *soundbites* - quotations that will make the article fun or compelling to read. At the end, give contact details for the public and a contact name and phone number where the journalist can reach the press co-ordinator of the event.

Make sure your press release is double spaced and printed in black ink. You can post press releases but it's much better to fax them to the news desk. Sometimes press releases in the post are binned before they reach the relevant person.

The national press are generally not interested in animal rights news and events and you'll need the help of professional journalists to get into these papers because they always have far more stories than they can print. Some national animal rights charities have experienced journalists writing their press releases and know the style that will appeal to each of the big papers. The success rate of getting into these papers is not as high as for locals, but the impact can be enormous when over a million people see even a very short piece.

They will often run a story on a special event such as National Vegetarian Week, especially if celebrity quotes and pictures are available. At such times, **you can get a local angle on this by linking up with the national organisation and getting your name put on the press releases that they will send to all the press, including your local papers.**

The local papers will ask you why you became a vegetarian, what your family think, what do you buy and how do you cook it, and what people can do to follow in your footsteps. If you have a local event running at the same time, such as a cookery demonstration, there's a good chance they'll send a photographer too.

If your paper has a 'What's On' section, send them details of all your meetings and planned events. Even if they don't use everything you send, they'll remember you. **Next time a story breaks about animals, they may phone you up for your expert comments.** This applies to radio and TV too.

For example, stories about Animal Liberation Front actions are usually ignored because the papers have been asked by the police not to print them as "they encourage more of the same". But if they do decide to print a story on, for example, an arson attack on a meat distributor, and ask for your comments to contrast with those of the owner, you can safely say something like:

"Our group is completely law-abiding and we would never condone illegal activities. But let me explain why these people feel that the meat industry is evil and why they did this. Two million animals are killed every day in Britain for food that isn't even healthy. Many of them are fully conscious when slaughtered.

"Their entire lives were spent indoors in factory farms in cramped conditions, and they are fed hormones and pumped full of drugs to try to cure all the diseases that such overcrowding and stress causes."

Never forget that over issues such as this they are not usually looking for truth or objectivity. They could be looking to "do a job" on you. Think carefully about what you intend to say and do not be drawn into saying something which can be misinterpreted.

Never say anything "off the record" to a journalist.

If a fur shop has been targeted, you could say: "Our group campaigns using legal methods such as leafleting and demonstrations against the fur trade because we feel that it's totally sick that in the twenty first century, some people are still walking around in coats made from wild animals which have either been kept in tiny cages all their lives and then gassed or strangled, or caught in gruesome 'leg-hold' traps which cause a slow, agonising death".

"Decades of campaigning have almost got rid of the fur trade in this country, but there are still some shops selling fur and we can understand why some people feel driven to try and put them out of business for good."

GETTING ON THE RADIO

As well as writing to the local papers, send press releases to your local radio stations. They also are always looking for stories with a local angle - you! If you have a good knowledge of all the issues, **then offer to go on the radio for a phone-in or discussion about going vegetarian.**

You can talk about your own story, reaction of family and friends, what to say to schoolmates or workmates, what you eat and how to cook it. You could even take some food into the studio.

Going on radio is very exciting and not too scary because it's just you and a presenter in the studio. It's okay if you "fluff" your lines a bit at first. They may simply arrange to interview you on the phone, in which case they'll call you a few minutes before going on air. You'll be able to hear the program down the line and the presenter will bring you in to have your say.

Preparation is vital! The leaflets and guides produced by national organizations contain good answers to all the standard questions that have been tried and tested. We strongly recommend that you get all the Viva! guides and Vegan Society leaflets and get to know them well, and the other factsheets recommended in the Resources sections.

Being interviewed is like taking an oral exam in animal rights - easy but only if you're well prepared. Memorise the points in these and your own leaflets so that you're ready for anything. As before any exam, read through the day before and practise your key points.

Always ask who else is to be interviewed, the format of the programme, how your contribution will be used and what the focus of the programme is to be. Always have three important points you want to communicate and try to get them in. Use the presenter's questions to say what <u>you</u> want to say, don't allow them to control the agenda and don't allow them to push you onto the defensive. The moment you do that, you've lost it. If in doubt, listen to a politician being interviewed to learn how it's really done!

If you know that there will be a devious representative of the Meat and Livestock Commission (MLC) or the National Farmers' Union (NFU) on the same program, then you really must know what you're talking about. Make sure you're up to date on the issues for discussion. Be ready with answers to all their standard lines (or is it lies?) about protein, iron, meat being necessary as part of a balanced diet, calcium, B12, vegetarians being short of things, "We have the highest standards in Europe" and the usual drivel these public relations experts excrete. If you prepare throughly, you can have them for breakfast every time.

Before going up against government or academic types, practise taking turns with a friend interviewing each other, increasing the speed and intensity. If they say something you don't know the answer to, do what they do all the time, just ignore it and make one of your points. Keep talking and get as many points in as you can. After the broadcast, people won't remember that you lost a couple of points, but they will remember the new information you gave them about factory farming, nutrition and health, and they may try their local health food shop or get more info from you.

Always finish by telling them what they can do for animals and where to get more information and advice.

Finally, be ready for the trick question at the end like "Well that's fascinating, but tell me, what do you think of people committing acts of violence in the cause of animal rights?" Or, "So you're saying that your aim is to put all our livestock farmers out of business?" which can come as a nasty surprise... unless of course you've done your homework!

TELEVISION

Don't miss out your local TV stations. Your hit rate with them will be lower, but the coverage will be brilliant. Local TV often pick up a story which has appeared in the papers. Again, before going on TV, practise what you'll say by getting a friend to test you hard and then swapping roles.

Ask the same questions as you would for radio. Local TV will almost certainly pre-record a lot of material, re-shoot anything they're not happy with and edit it to just a short piece with the best bits. There's really nothing to be afraid of and it is brilliant seeing your group on the News. However, **their aim is often to make you look radical or threatening so protect yourself. If it's a documentary, again ask all the questions about editorial focus, who else is appearing, how your contributions will be used - and get the answers in writing!**

Finally, when you do get into the media, some people might accuse you of being more interested in promoting yourself than in promoting animal rights. The truth is that in the process of publicising the facts about animal cruelty, it is inevitable that people will be seen in the media and those watching will remember those who turned them on to animal rights.

Remember, preaching to the converted won't change much. Preaching to the convertible will - and the best way to reach the 90% of people who aren't even vegetarian yet is through the mainstream media.

Go for it!

The Power of the Internet

Almost as soon as the internet was developed, campaigners began to see its potential for ideas and information sharing. It is no exaggeration to say that during the last few years the internet has become one of the most effective tools available to campaigners.

The internet is amazing in that it allows us to effortlessly cross the barriers of time and distance. Campaigners from all over the world can now send large amounts of important information to each other within seconds, for virtually no cost!

Campaigning organisations now produce colourful websites which are packed with information and very easy to use. We can all access this information from anywhere in the world, at any time of the day or night.

Within the last couple of years, the internet has been used to plan and promote large scale national demonstrations. This has boosted the turnout at some high profile events and brought thousands of new campaigners into the movement for social change.

As we stated earlier in this chapter, any media coverage for our campaigns is an asset to us, but our pro-animal message is frequently censored and distorted by the media and this can set us back in our campaigning and alienate us from the public.

Using the internet however, we can at last take control of how we promote our ideas. We can free ourselves from damaging media stereotypes and say exactly what we want to the whole world. We can make our own media!

We urge all campaigners to get on-line. Not only will you then be able to look up websites, but you can subscribe to forums and e-mailing lists and have totally up to date news and information sent to you on a daily basis.

We are living in the midst of a communication revolution. The internet gives us opportunities that previous generations never had. It is our duty to seize these opportunities and use them in our struggle to bring about a more compassionate world.

Getting On-Line for Beginners

Choosing a computer, modem, Internet service provider and browser is like choosing a car. Basically they all do the job. Questions to consider are cost, do they give 24 hour support on line and by telephone, do they charge for support, can you access your email in other countries.

Quite honestly, if you're a beginner, it doesn't make a lot of difference who you sign up with. **Find out what your friends use and choose the same then you'll be sorted for support**, as most Internet providers either offer little help or it's shut at the sort of times you surf, or you can't get through, or they charge premium phone rates by the minute. Whereas your mates will already have solved whatever problems you might encounter.

Some ISP's (internet service providers) such as Freeserve offer **free connection** to the internet but you pay for phone calls and they get a commission from the telephone company.

Other ISP's such as America On Line (AOL) offer free phone calls for a **fixed monthly charge**, which can work out cheaper if you're on line a lot. If your ISP offers you several screen names for one account, then other people in your house (or elsewhere) can connect using your account, each of you with your own private email box, though only one of you can be on line at any one time.

For a free email forwarding account that works anywhere in the world, try **www.hotmail.com** or **www.bigfoot.com**. The advantage over many of the free services provided by other companies is that you're not locked into a single browser, which can be a major problem when you stay with friends in another city for a month, or go abroad and try to retrieve your email from a cybercafe in northern Thailand that doesn't have a copy of your browser.

For a good browser, the software that lets you look at websites on the net, everyone gets a copy of **Internet Explorer** with their PC. **Outlook Express** is good, it can divert incoming emails into particular directories which is wonderful if you get a lot of emails you want to keep.

Ronny uses Bigfoot as she rarely stays in the same place for long and is always using other people's computers.

Alex uses America On Line which is easy, with unlimited access for a fixed fee, and unlike some free ISP's growing too quickly you don't ever lose emails and you can always get connected, but he has a back up hotmail account which at the time of writing offers some facilities for receiving certain kinds of complex emails (with multiple attachments) more easily than in AOL. A very nice browser is **Opera**, which you can download from www.opera.com. In the end, one tv set is much like another, it's what's showing inside the frame that you're really interested in.

Finding Information On-Line

There are plenty of places to start. Check out our list of websites in the **Resources** chapter 16 or in the online version of this book at **www.CampaignAgainstCruelty.co.uk**, and look at **www.yahoo.com** (under Society and Culture, Animal Rights) or try **www.excite.com** (under Lifestyle, Pets and Animals, Animal Rights). Most sites have a page of links to other sites. After you get your next phone bill you may then consider unlimited access.

Building a website

Once you've figured out email and surfed a few of the funky vegsites, it's time to put up a page about what you're up to. The easiest way is to use the free software **FrontPage Express** from Microsoft, but then you have to figure out how it works. Ronny particularly recommends **Dreamweaver**. You can also find sites that help you to make your own site. Try www.moonfruit.com.

Every bookshop has hundreds of **books** about the web, most of them too advanced or too simple. Alex, who used to be a programmer and a computer science lecturer, highly recommends the book *Teach Yourself to Create Web Pages in 24 Hours* by Ned Snell, published by Sams, which includes a diskette with FrontPage Express on it.

You'll also need some hard disk space at an Internet Service Provider (ISP) to store your site. You can get free webspace in many places, perhaps with your email account you may get 10MB, but you may be stuck with the provider's adverts on your site and there will be a limit on how many people can view it.

For example you can register for a free email account with www.freeserve.co.uk and they will give you free web space. Or try www.geocities.com for heavy duty access. This is a good place to put up a free homepage about your group or yourself. If you build a serious site, once you get it working **it's worth paying a little to get space that you control fully without adverts and that has more bandwidth**, which refers to how fast it can transfer data or how many people can access it at the same time. As with choosing your ISP, ask other groups what they use and then they can help you get started if you're bamboozled by all the techno-jargon.

If you have products like a veggie guide to your town, T-shirts, tickets for coaches to demos etc, you may want to open a shop on line. First you must contact your bank to arrange to be able to take credit cards, and this could cost you a set up fee plus a monthly charge. Or check out sites like worldpay.com who collect money for you online for a commission. Then you'll need the software to run a shop.

Some companies will build and host a shop for you for a fixed fee per month, but if you work out what this fee adds up to over a few years you may be in for a bit of a shock. A cheaper way is to buy the software for a shop, work through the manual, and build it yourself. Alex went to computer trade and ebusiness shows, looked at lots of packages and chose Actinic (from www.actinic.co.uk), which has different versions according to how many products you sell and whether you want to offer wholesale or foreign currency.

Pictures can really make a website look exciting, but they greatly increase the time it takes for people to download your page. A recent study claims that most people will, on average, wait for a maximum of eight seconds for a page to download before losing interest and going elsewhere.

Keep any pictures you use small, perhaps a square inch or less in size, and limit the number of colours. Use photos saved as JPEG files and cartoon artwork saved as GIF files so that the image is compressed. Scanning at 72 dots per inch (dpi) gives a good resolution on big pictures stored as JPEG files but is slow to load, so try scanning at 24dpi or 36dpi and using a smaller image on the screen.

If your images are around 7 kilobytes then they load quickly and net surfers can always click on the small image to go to a page with a big version, as you can see for example with the book covers at amazon.com. 1,000 characters of text takes up 1KB and downloads very quickly. A 1,000 x 1,000 pixel picture in colour could take several minutes to download!

The internet is the life blood of the animal rights movement. It cannot be censored or blockaded or closed by the police or government. It links us all together to form one massive global movement for social change.

Just as cheap computers and printing created true freedom of the press, so the arrival of **broad band access and digital tv will allow us in a few years to launch animal rights video channels with a global audience. If you think the internet is impressive now, believe us, you ain't seen nothin' yet.**

Getting on line and finding your way around the net means investing a few weeks in figuring out how it works. It's easy if you have a friend to coach you and it gives you a phenomenally powerful set of tools to join in the global vegolution as a teacher or peace warrior. Don't give up if you get stuck, just pick up the phone and call a friend for help, then pass it down the line when you get proficient.

The truth is out there on the net, and it's a vital part of creating a vegan world. In our lifetimes.

chapter eight

YOUR GROUP NEWSLETTER

*"Without a journal of some kind
you cannot unite a community." - Gandhi*

To make everyone in your group feel involved, put everything that your group has done or plans to do in your own newsletter.

This is great for people who can't make it to meetings, and new members can read the back issues to get a full picture of the group's recent history.

The newsletter will pre-empt a lot of questions at meetings, so that they can focus on planning and decision making. Looking back on past issues will give a real sense of achievement to the group. For a superb example of what can be done, check out the London Animal Action Newsletter.

The Editor

One person must take responsibility for editing the Newsletter. It's usually quite easy to choose this bod, because it's a big job requiring excellent English, free time, access to a computer, and the ability to totally rewrite some articles that ramble.

If you have more than one person in the group who can and wants to do this, consider yourselves unique. However the more people can help with typing, cartoons, copying and distribution, the better.

What to Include

The Editor gets reports from members of whatever you think will interest the group. This can be summaries of what you've been doing and plan to do, a calendar of coming events, press cuttings from other animal rights magazines and national papers, cartoons, and articles by members about anything to do with animal rights.

Try to avoid articles about feeding goldfish and stick to a mixture of useful stuff for new converts such as recipes (which should always be vegan), and inspiring and uplifting reports for campaigners.

An easy way to fill space is to photocopy articles directly from other mags... but that's pretty boring. A more interesting venture is to ask members to contribute something that they know a lot about based on their beliefs or experience:

> A Day In The Life of a Sabber
> How I Converted My Mum to Veganism
> A Survey of Wholefood Shops in Our Town
> The day we organised a Benefit Gig

Other staple fare are book reviews, reports on ongoing national campaigns, news of new products in the local shops, and Freepost addresses and Freephone numbers of animal abusing organizations. We believe this is for information only, so that your supporters can complain to companies about their dodgy pratises at their expense, though someone did once say something about bricks being very heavy.

You can also ask local ethical businesses to donate some money in return for advertising, or to sell your newsletter in their shops.

How to Write a Fun Article

Imagine you're sitting with a friend explaining how you eat. Or you're in the kitchen together, or at the shops. What would you say to her? Imagine how you speak when you're feeling happy and excited at being with someone who wants to copy you. Hear yourself speaking. Now write down what you're saying to her. Write down everything you can think of about the subject. If you know it, your readers need to know it too or they will not understand as well as you do.

Now rewrite by cutting. Don't use a paragraph to say what can be said in a sentence. Most of the words are unnecessary. Cut, cut, cut. Then cut some more. Make every word count.

Look again at what you've written. All the essential information is there. But is it fun to read? If you want to hold the attention of a pre-vegetarian then, like a popular magazine, you have to make it exciting or funny.

You have to make people want to read because what you say is entertaining. When you're writing about very serious issues you can be serious. But when you're writing about life as a vegan, make sure you include plenty of fun or love or whatever is most important to you.

Structure of your Newsletter

For some sections of your newsletter, choose a title:

Campaigns Corner
The Big Interview
A.R. Calendar
Feeding Frenzy
Quote of the Month.

This gives a theme to draw people back every issue to their favourite pages. How many people buy Viz every month just because they adore a certain character? It may not be your cup of herb tea, but it's a standard way to keep the content consistantly interesting while introducing new subjects.

For each article, list the points you believe are important. Use bold letters or boxes to draw the reader's attention to key points, to seduce them into reading the article now.

PRODUCTION

"Freedom of the press exists for anyone who can afford a press."

Suppose you've just been landed with the job of doing next month's newsletter. Oh cripes, what to do next? How much does it cost to produce a newsletter? What do you need? Here are some ideas:

        A. lots of time
        B. a word processor and printer
        C. some money to pay for typesetting
        D. more money to pay for illustrations
        E. lots of money to pay for printing

Oh dear. This looks like it's going to be very expensive. But in fact you don't need any of the above things to produce a newsletter. The only thing you must have is imagination. We're going to tell you how to make the the most of whatever resources you have, even if you have almost NO time or NO money.

Here is a key idea. If you have a good idea, you will always find other people who want to help you. In fact if you want to do anything significant, you will normally need to work with others. That's one of the reasons for starting a groups, so that we can find people to help us.

Everything that now exists started as an idea. You now have an idea for a newsletter. There are some problems ahead, but you've spent your entire life solving problems. There isn't a single problem involved in producing a newsletter that you cannot resolve. Especially now that you're part of a local group linked to the national and international animal rights community.

Whatever your situation, it has advantages and disadvantages. There is no strength without weakness, and no weakness without strength. So let's look at your situation.

A. Time

Perhaps you have four children, a job, and no time or energy. Then find ways to make some time, and find people to help you! Can you really not afford to give up one or two evenings of goggle-box watching to help change the world?

There are sure to be people in your group with heaps of free time to help you. Find out who's unemployed, who are the school and college students, and who's retired. If you work in an office, try taking a writing break instead of a coffee break. It's also amazing how much you can do in half an hour, or an hour after work.

B. Finding a Word Processor

If you're unemployed you may not have much money. But you are in the perfect position to write, because you already have the one thing that most people want - TIME. So start writing now.

Do you know a vegetarian secretary or a student? Every office or college has computers which your friend could use. Almost certainly a student friend can take you into her university or college and show you how to use a word processor there.

Do you know any children? Do any of them have a computer? Can you ask them to show you the word processor? Do you have a friend who has a computer? Could you use it one or two evenings per week, or on a Sunday?

Perhaps you work where there are computers which you can use for typing during your lunch hour. Or maybe you could arrive a little early in the morning or leave late one evening per week? Even if it's too dangerous to do your own work in the office, perhaps you can use the nice printer for work that you've typed at home or in a friend's house.

Perhaps your group has enough money to buy a cheap old Amstrad computer out of the paper for under £100. This will be fine for inputting the text of articles. Later you can transfer it to a more expensive computer to turn it into the finished product. Just make sure you get a PC with a 3.5" diskette, not a PCW with 3" drives that is incompatible with everything else around these days. Or much better still try blagging an old 286 or 386 or best of all 486 computer from someone who's just upgraded to a shiny new Pentium.

C. Typesetting

Typesetting is the process of taking a document and making it look like this book, or better. However remember the phrase "The best is the enemy of the good." If your newsletter contains useful information, then start publishing it now and worry about the presentation later.

If you have a friend with a powerful computer that can do typesetting, ask about using the computer for your book. Professional typesetting is expensive. But if you can get it for nothing, then go for it. Strangely enough, most people with computers just love showing off what they can do, and they can do your typesetting in the process!

The standard package for typesetting on PC's these days is Quark Xpress. But you can do some pretty impressive stuff with much cheaper software such as Pagemaker, Microsoft Publisher or Lotus Wordpro (formerly called Amipro), or even with Microsoft Word or Wordperfect, and these will run quite happily on cheaper 386 or possibly even 286 computers. Contact any groups whose newsletters you like for their tips. They might even lend you a copy of their software to try it out.

D. Illustrations

Your newsletter will look much nicer with a few pictures. These can be very simple, and you can draw them yourself. Ask around if anyone is an artist. If you see a picture you like in an animal rights magazine, ask if you can use it. (Most people don't bother to ask, but we thought we'd better tell you anyway.)

E. Printing

Now this is the expensive part, right? Wrong! It is possible to print your newsletter without spending much money at all. After the tenth draft on a home bubblejet printer, what now?

Before we tell you how to print for nothing, let's discuss the size of your newsletter. The normal size of paper in a printer is A4 (30cm x 21cm). This is much too big for a small publication, so we suggest you use A5 (21cm x 15cm), which is half the size. Print A4 and photocopy reduce two pages together onto an A4 sheet for folding.

Now, what about free printing? Let's imagine that you've produced your Newsletter and you're ready to print. How many copies do you need? One hundred, one thousand, or maybe ten thousand? How do you eliminate the risk of printing too many? By printing only as many as you know you need. So print them using a photocopier.

You will need to borrow or buy a big stapler, at least 15cm long. This is your major investment, but it will be good for years. Students can often buy photocopying cards at cheap prices to use in their library. And photocopy shops near universities can be much cheaper than in the centre of town.

Some people have photocopied at work in the evenings, especially if they work for the government and believe they should have some compensation for all the tax subsidies that go to the meat and milk industries and the hospitals full of sick meat eaters. Not to mention the fact that there's nothing they can eat in the canteen. But of course we wouldn't dream of irresponsibly and illegally telling you to do something dangerous or illegal. So don't even think of doing this. Okay?

Personally we think it's best not to print more than a few dozen mags at a time. You may pay twice as much per 'zine as if you print 100, but you eliminate the risks of spending too much too soon. After all, if you sell all 25 quickly and need to reprint, is that really a problem? One famous entrepreneur used to say "Look after the down side, and the upside will take care of itself."

As we go to press, a new development has radically reduced the cost of laser printing. Previously laser printers used to cost hundreds of pounds, and you'd get stitched up for even more for the drums and toner cartridges. And they weren't very environmentally friendly. But they were super-fast compared to inkjet printers.

Laser printers are now cheap, but you still pay more than the cost of the printer over its lifetime by having to keep replacing the drum. Kyocera Ecosys laser printers, like the FS-600 we used to produce this book, have drums that last virtually forever so you only have to pay for ink. The cost of a toner cartridge is £30 or less, so that's about a penny a page and you have a printing press at home.

WHAT ABOUT MARKETING?

Peter Cox, the author of *Why You Don't Need Meat* which has sold over 100 000 copies, said, "I've never met an intelligent person who, when presented with the arguments didn't become a vegetarian."

On the other hand, Robin Webb, the British ALF Press Officer, once said "American research shows that 88% of the population are only interested in their own little family grouping. You're wasting your time with them."

Listen to criticism, but don't let anyone stop you from doing what you believe in.

There are two kinds of magazine you can produce: one for the general public, and one for group members only. Here we'll talk about promoting your magazine to Joe or Joanna Public.

So just how do you sell your magazine to the people who are ready to buy it, without wasting time and money on the others? Here are some ideas for marketing without paying for advertising.

First of all, always carry some copies with you, especially when you go to anything involving animal rights or green people. Everyone will be interested in the newsletters you are carrying in your hand. Let them take one away for half an hour to read. Many of them will come back and say "This is great, I want one. How much is it?"

Send copies to the local newspaper and radio stations, especially vegetarian journalists. Ask them to review it and tell people to order from you.

Take your newsletter to local vegetarian cafes, wholefood shops, "hippy" shops, community centres and anywhere that gets a subsidy from the Council. Give them some copies on "sale or return" and a photocopy of any magazine reviews. Ask them to suggest other shops. Stick one in the Library. Amazingly enough, pet shops are also sometimes good. They're sometimes run by well-meaning "we love animals" types who'll say "Oh it's about animals, we'll take some." (Unless of course you've put an exposé of the pet trade on the cover!)

How Much to Charge

Business types will tell you to charge as much as the market can support. Other people will tell you that AR stuff should be as cheap as possible. What should you do?

There is not much point in producing a local general circulation magazine if you lose money. You will need to pay for stamps and phone calls, photocopying, and later for printing and possibly advertising, but really it can't be too cheap. If you can get enough advertising to give it away, then you're really in business.

There's a fantastic green, ethical and vegetarian newspaper called Satya available free in New York, paid for by a handful of advertisements. It's produced by newspaper professionals. We hope to see ethical newspapers popping up in every city in the future in this country too.

A WORD OF WARNING

Finally, and more sinisterly, if a group does not have a newsletter or magazine that frankly reports everything that's going on, then there's a real danger that one or two ambitious people could one day take over. They withhold information as a way of exerting control. They hold closed committee meetings in secret and publish only as much as the law requires to give an illusion of democracy. And they expel or refuse membership to anyone who tries to blow the whistle on them. We've seen this happen time and again in local groups and at least three national organizations. So be warned! If your newsletter doesn't contain full details of decisions made in meetings, somebody may have something to hide.

FINAL TIPS

Keep a note book in your pocket or bag and by your bed.

Contact your friends and ask them to help.

Look in the libary for a book about journalism or sub-editing.

Find people with word processors and start typing.

Visit photocopy shops, libraries and printers.

Keep a folder full of useful info and press-cuttings to quote from in articles.

If you've found these notes helpful, please send us a copy of your newsletter!

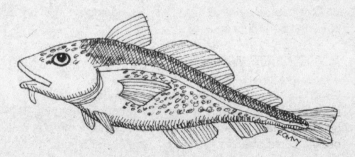

chapter nine

DISPLAYS AND EXHIBITIONS

"A picture paints a thousand words."

You can put on a display in any public place, such as a library, entrance to a civic building, hospital, university, catering college, school, or as part of a larger exhibition. It's very cheap and easy to do, and requires almost no maintenance. The same display can be reused and improved over the years to come.

The simplest display is some posters and leaflets stuck on a wall. Aim to use lots of photos and big pictures, and the odd chart or graph, and go easy on detailed writing.

Aim to get people's attention with photos and cartoons and give them enough food for thought to get some literature or take some action, or at the very least sow seeds of understanding, empathy and compassion.

Display boards are very nice, but unfortunately very expensive also. A small set costs hundreds of pounds. See if you can scrounge some for your display from a charity or someone else who does displays.

Alternatively, make your own by buying (or scrounging, if you are lucky) some large pieces of strong, light wood, roughly 2m by 1m. Cover each one with thick, tear-resistant material, preferably unpatterned and dark in colour. Then join them together with hinges, two or three to each join.

Use a word processor or coloured pens to make captions for photos and drawings, and to make big headings for each section of your display. Different coloured paper can be used for each section, and you can use bigs sheets of paper as a background. If someone can draw or knows about design, get them involved.

Go easy with text. Lots of leaflets with small writing will be hard work to read. Cut out the pictures and type the best bits again in big letters, or put the leaflets as a small part of the display for those who have time or inclination to read in detail. People can always come back later for another look.

GOOD TOPICS ARE:

Live exports. Show the separation from mothers and say that the animals cry for days, the facts about overcrowding, distance, stress, dead on arrivals. Show the veal crates in France that have been illegal in Britain since 1990. Next, and this is the good bit, **explain how all this is caused by people drinking milk** and then explain the alternatives and how to make them or buy them locally.

Vegetarianism. Do displays on the main reasons that meat is bad: factory farms, slaughter, health, waste of land. Then, or next to each section, **show the alternatives.** Give ideas of what folk can do to wash their hands of meat, and the benefits to them and nature.

Veganism. Do displays on egg farming, including so-called free range with pictures of male chicks being gassed and crushed, and show what happens to old chickens. Do the same for milk and veal, and draw attention to the death of the dairy cow at only 7 years instead of 20. Show vegan foods such as the **new four food groups:** grains, pulses, fruit,

vegetables. You can find out more about this at
www.pcrm.org. The new four food groups are not to be
confused with the (old) four food groups of the Health
Education Council, still promoted in British schools although
abolished in America after lobbying by doctors, which consider
dairy (or dairy and soya products) an essential food group;
which is, of course, complete and utter tosh.

Vegetarian Food. The new four food groups - you can get
charts from Physicians Committee for Responsible Medicine
or The American Vegan Society. How to cook beans.
Different kinds of bean and products made from soya. Meat
replacers like TVP and Cheatin' Ham. Using herbs, spices,
soy sauce, garlic and lemon juice. Vegetarian dishes of the
great cuisines: India, China, Japan (macrobiotics), Turkey,
Mexico, Italy, Middle East.

Heart Disease. Charts showing 50% of meat eaters die of
heart disease, 25% of vegetarians, 4% of vegans. Diagrams
of the heart and what happens when arteries fur up. What
causes furring up. Where saturated fat and cholesterol come
from. Foods that are full of fat and sodium. Cholesterol and
low fat foods. Why switching from beef to chicken makes
almost no difference. Why switching to beans does. Why
non-smoking vegans rarely get heart disease. Plant foods
with no cholesterol and low fat. Dr Dean Ornish's diet for
reversing heart disease.
(You can get the facts from Dr Klaper's books and videos.)

Ecology. Get facts from *The Silent Ark*, McLibel literature,
and Viva! guides. Draw graphics of how many people a field
can feed on different diets. Say there ae 25 billion acres of
farmland in the world and a meat eater needs 3 acres,
whereas a vegan needs 1/4 acre. In the next century
population will pass 10 billion. Uh oh! Animal farm effluent
causes half of water pollution. Deforestation for beef. Cow
farts are potent greenhouse gases. Topsoil loss. Third world
poverty and meat.

Nutrition. The six things you need: carbohydrates, protein, fat, vitamins, minerals, water. The things you don't need like cholesterol, pesticides, BSE. The different food groups and what they contain. What is a balanced diet. Cooked or raw. Major western causes of death and how animal foods cause them. Different diets: omnivore, veggie, vegan, macrobiotic, raw food, fruitarian. Deficiency myths about vegans: protein, calcium, iron, B12. Good sources are Peter Cox's Encyclopedia of Vegetarian Living, Vegan Nutrition, and anything by Dr Klaper.

National Vegetarian Week (June) or **World Vegan Day** (1st November). Get posters and leaflets from the nationals, and add your own recipes, pictures of celebrity vegetarians, where to get food in your town. Before and after foods like burger/veggieburger. At the end of your display, put the addresses where people can get more info and ask them to send at least a stamp (unless they're very young). If your budget stretches to it, put some leaflets on a table.

Case study

HOW TO WIN PEOPLE'S MINDS

by Swiss activist Sigrid De Leo, fulltime teacher and Secretary of the European Vegetarian Union.

I went to the headteacher of the local high school, with 400 students aged 15-20, and asked him whether he would agree to an exhibition "Vegetarianism and Health" in the entrance hall of the school. He agreed on the condition that we would not include publicity for particular products like tofu.

Together with the Swiss Vegetarian Association (SVV) we covered nine poster boards (180cm x 180cm) on both sides with posters. The subjects were: general health, environment, animal welfare, religion and ethics, politics, economics famous vegetarians, quotations of famous vegetarians and prejudices.

As well as the written posters, we displayed several photoposters showing fresh fruit and vegetables, and pictures of hens, pigs and cows in dreadful conditions in factory farms. There was a poster in which little pigs were castrated, obviously without anaesthetic, and a big poster with a clean, intelligent looking pig saying "My flesh belongs to me. If you want to eat meat, bite into your own arse."

Some examples of what we have displayed:

1. General Health: the results of longterm studies on vegetarians; statistics on the growing consumption of meat compared to the growing number of diseases. Anatomical comparison of carnivores and fruitarians. Statements and quotations of professors of medicine. Physical and mental fitness. Nutrition and allergies. Iron. Protein.

2. Environment: the consequences of factory farming on soil, water, climate, acid rain, third world.

3. Animal welfare: "Humane slaughter", "Could we not bring up animals without suffering" and other popular misconceptions.

4. Religion and Ethics: quotations from the Bible. The Bible and vegetarianism. Christian religion. General quotations from priests.

5. Politics and Economy: comparison of subsidies for meat and plant production.

6. Famous vegetarians: quotations from Aristotle, Thomas Edison, R. W. Emerson, Gandhi, Aldous Huxley, Rousseau, George Bernard Shaw, Isaac Bashevis Singer, Rudolf Steiner, Henry David Thoreau, Leo Tolstoy and Voltaire.

7. Prejudices: "They are only animals," "Humans have always eaten meat", "Humans come first", "Humans are biologically meat-eaters", "I cannot change anything", "Animals eat one another too" and other myths.

Newspapers and the local radio reported the exhibition. We estimate that its message reached nearly two hundred thousand people. For two weeks there were always crowds of people reading or discussing near the posterwalls. There was not a lesson during the two weeks that the students did not discuss with their teachers the vegetarian way of life. I was approached by mothers who asked me what to cook, because their son or daughter would not eat meat any more after seeing the exhibition.

We are translating all the materials into English, so if anybody has an opportunity to organize an exhibition in a school, university, youth centre or shopping centre, we would gladly pass on our documentation. Just write or give us a call.

Sigrid De Leo, EVU Secretary, Bluetschwitzerweg 5, 9443 Widnau, Switzerland. Tel/Fax +41-71-722 64 45. Email: evu@openoffice.ch

chapter ten

SPEAKING TO SCHOOLS AND OTHER GROUPS

Speaking in schools is important work. Young people are often more able to relate to new ideas and opinions than adults because their minds are more active and questioning. Don't forget that today's teenagers are tomorrow's parents, employers and teachers.

Teenagers are surrounded by exciting, fashionable images. You need to bear this in mind if you want to grab their attention and hold it long enough to get your message through. It's no good simply reciting a list of facts and figures, you need to make the subject 'come alive', or your young audience will switch off. You need to promote animal rights issues as important, sensible and modern.

PREPARATION

This is essential. If you turn up ready to give your talk confident that you can explain your subject as you go along, you will be in for a shock. Ronny has made this mistake herself and knows what it feels like to come unstuck in this way! You need to sit down for a few hours with a selection of books, lots of scrap paper and an inspiring friend.

Work out the objective of the talk. Is it about animal rights in general?, bloodsports?, responsible pet care? veganism/vegetarianism? The chances are that the teacher you contact in order to arrange the talk will have specific ideas about the subject matter, because they will want to relate your talk to the current sujects the class are studying. The vegetarian diet is part of the national curriculum for schools, so this is probably what the teacher will want you to talk about. Make certain you know what the teacher's requirements are. You can't just talk about anything you like.

Work out the essential message which your audience should be left with, eg. 'there are lots of arguments against eating meat and it is easier than you thought to give it up.'

PLANNING YOUR TALK

Once you are concentrating fully on this, list the points you want to make. Write anything that comes into your head, no matter how trivial it seems.

Then go through these points, scribbling out any which you change your mind about. Arrange these points under general headings, for example;

Animal rights - unnatural, crowded living conditions, painful slaughter, killed at young age, use of growth hormones
Environment - pollution, waste of land, deforestation
Human rights - third world starvation
Diet - meat is unhealthy, an animal-free diet can be healthy and fun

Work out how you are going to structure your talk. Which issue should come first? How will you explain each issue as you go along? How will you motivate your audience to take action? How will you use visual aids to back up what you are saying. Can you make use of an overhead projector, slides or better still, a video? (see resources chapter)

Then write your talk. Edit and re-edit until it feels right. Keep asking your friend for advice and pay attention to what they say. Something which sounds witty and persuasive to you might sound really naff to them.

If you know any teenagers, read your talk out to them and ask them their honest opinion. Check that your talk is the right length. Speak slowly and clearly and time yourself. Otherwise you could end up either rushing through your talk in a flustered state or waffling desperately. Fifteen minutes is a good length of time to aim for. The teacher will probably advise you on the expected length of the talk.

During your talk, you will need to make sure that your audience fully understand what you are saying or you will be wasting your time. Assume that your audience have no prior knowledge of animal cruelty, but don't patronise them by talking to them as if they are stupid. The tone needs to be just right.

You can explain complicated issues quite simply if you paint pictures with your words. If you say, "imagine if a hundred of you were suddenly crowded onto a school bus with no seats and driven around for two days with no stops for refreshments or the toilet and you were given no explanation about why you were being treated that way. Imagine how uncomfortable, frightened and upset you would all feel. That's what it must be like for animals being transported abroad."...

...you will immediately encourage your audience to relate the suffering of animals to their worst nightmares. You will gain their understanding and sympathy. Simply saying, "imagine a hundred sheep being transported a long distance in a lorry with no food or water," will not have anything like the same effect.

After you have finished talking, it is important to open up the discussion by asking your audience if they have any questions. This will be the most nerve-wracking part of all if you haven't done the necessary preperation. In every audience there is always at least one 'smart arse' who is determined to try and make you look stupid. Teenagers can be experts at this! Assume that there will be such a character in your audience. Consider all the possible questions which they could come up with. What we suggest is that you and your friend write down a list of these questions, then consider each one in turn and come up with a short, smart answer to it.

Delivery

When you actually come to give your talk, pay attention to your appearence, most of all your clothes. If you walk in in a grey suit, your audience will be bored before you open your mouth. If you dress up in your most outrageous clothes, they will think you are weird. Clothes say a lot about a person and if you want your audience to like what you say, you must make sure they like the way you look. We suggest you wear clothes which are relatively fashionable, but which you feel comfortable in.

You can choose whether to stand or sit while you give the talk. Most people feel more comfortable sitting down and there is no point in making yourself feel uncomfortable or you will start to become nervous. If you sit, make sure you sit upright.

Don't place a barrier between you and the audience. It is better to sit on a desk that at a chair behind it. Consider your body language. Make sure that you appear relaxed and open, not closed and defensive. Keep your hands relaxed, your shoulders wide and your feet still. Avoid fidgeting as this will distract your audience and possibly irritate them.

The way you talk is as important as what you actually say. Working class kids won't be impressed if you try too hard to sound like a BBC evening news reader. Remember that you are giving the talk because you have strong views about animal rights and you want your audience to be influenced by your views. Don't speak in a flat monotone, use your voice to express your feelings of concern, anger, humour and encouragement. Be careful though to avoid going over the top, or it will seem as if you are making fun of your subject. You are a campaigner, not a stand up comedian!

Eye contact is essential. If you read your talk word for word from pages of notes, you will appear intimidating or amateur. It's best to memorise your talk beforehand and then take cue cards along with you on the day, on which you have written a summary of each argument. Arrange them in order. Glance at your first card to refresh your memory, talk about the topic, then move on to the next card and its topic. Continue until the end of your talk.

This method works like a DIY autocue and it ensures that you can maintain eye contact with your audience, yet not risk accidentally leaving out an important point.

When you finish speaking and come to invite questions from your audience, treat each question seriously and thank each person who asks a question. If you ridicule a question or refuse to answer it, you will appear aloof and smug and the audience will lose their respect for you. Don't worry about attention-seeking troublemakers. You won't be left alone with the kids. A teacher will be present and they will deal deal with such a pupil for you, by asking them to be quiet or sending them out of the room if necessary.

If you follow these points, your school talk will be a success and you will come away feeling elated and proud of yourself. This chapter is intended as an introduction to the subject.

If you are really keen to concentrate your efforts on school talks, we recommend that you send £2.50 to Viva! for a copy of their 'Guide to Speaking in Schools' pack. It is excellent and goes into a lot more detail about this subject. See resources section.

SUMMARY

1.) Be prepared
2.) Be careful about your appearence
3.) Relate to your audience
4.) Encourage participation
5.) Use visual aids
6.) Respect the views and needs of the teachers
7.) Relax and enjoy yourself

chapter eleven

PROMOTING VEGAN FOOD IN YOUR AREA

How to Get Ethical Food into Your Canteen

This section is for anyone whose university, college, school or workplace doesn't offer much for vegans and vegetarians in its canteens.

This was the situation at Bristol Polytechnic in 1990. Over a period of a few months, the student Animal Rights Group convinced the Polytechnic to offer acceptable meals. It took time, and we believe that by using the methods we discovered, it should be possible to get the same results anywhere.

"Thanks" to the Tories, canteens are now run as businesses. The manager will be afraid of a commercial disaster which would make her or him look bad and lose their contract. You can take advantage of this.

Your job is to show the canteen what a wonderful opportunity they have to increase sales. You must do this in a thorough and business-like fashion. Animal rights will cut no ice with them, and health not much more. This is an issue of choice, fulfilling their contractual obligation to cater to all customers, and increasing turnover.

Research Your Case

Go to the canteen and see what is there. Bite your tongue and resist the temptation to put anti-meat stickers everywhere.

Ask the chefs what they think about vegetarian food. You may get lucky and find that one of them has veggie tendencies.

Find out how many students are vegetarian or would like a vegetarian option in the canteen. Get figures from your national vegetarian society for the percentage of young people avoiding meat. In Britain you can say that 25% of women under 30 do not eat red meat, or 18% of students, and that these numbers are rising. You could do a survey of people going to the canteen. Even more importantly, find out what proportion of students do not eat there and find out why. This is a great project for marketing or economics students.

Make a CHOICE! petition, like the ones produced by Animal Aid and the Vegetarian Society which in the 80's got vegetarian food into almost every school in Britian. Take a standard petition form and at the top put something like "We the undersigned note that the canteen does not cater adequately or consistently for vegetarians and vegans and believe that a choice of vegetarian dishes and at least one vegan dish should be offered every day." Then get people to sign at a stall outside the canteen.

Find out if there is a **catering committee** for your college. At Bristol Poly, the committee was chaired by a lawyer who ensured that everyone got their point across fairly.

State Your Case in Writing

Write to the catering committee or whatever committee is responsible for the canteen. You need to write to allow time for the committee members to think about what you say. Also, by writing you force them to reply. Your job is not to convert the committee to vegetarianism, but to **present veggie dishes as a sound commercial decision**. Make the following points politely but firmly in about two pages:

X% of students in your country are vegetarian. This proportion is increasing. These students have the <u>right</u> to choose what they eat. The canteen has a monopoly on catering, and therefore an obligation to provide for them.

This is what the college is offering vegetarians: pizza made with cheese made with rennet from the stomachs of freshly killed calves, factory farmed eggs, fish, salads consisting of lettuce and tomatoes with no protein content. Say that this is not what you want!

Tell them that you want non-animal protein and wholefoods. Say that vegetarians like to replace animal proteins with beans, nuts and seeds. Many of us prefer long grain brown rice. We want salads with beans and nuts.

Remember, <u>don't</u> push the advantages of being a vegetarian, just **make it clear that this is what you, their clients, want**. You can say however that this kind of food is recommended in Health Education Council leaflets as a nutritionally superior replacement for animal products.

Say that vegan dishes have cheaper ingredients. Convince them that wholefood dishes will attract people who do not currently use the canteen.

Get the excellent Vegan Society catering pack for £1.95 and give it to the canteen. You could also try the Vegetarian Society (UK) for a copy of their catering pack, though the last time we rang up all we got was a brochure for their cookery school. You might be able to get a photocopy of it. Or arrange for the packs to be sent direct to the canteen manager.

Make sure they know however that many vegetarians will not eat the TVP (textured vegetable protein soya meat) suggested in the VSUK pack, though many meat eaters will. And point out that vegetarians are fed up with bloomin' cheese, cheese and cheese in every flippin' meal and it's the last thing they want to see!

At Bristol Polytechnic the chefs ordered ready made vegetarian meals. This was their idea. These meals are very expensive. They then used their professional expertise to clone the meals for a fraction of the cost. Suggest that your canteen does the same. They can offer vegetarian dishes on an experimental basis to see what the response is. If they don't like you, they may go along with it just to prove you wrong. Or the committee may force them to. They'll be in for a big surprise. Heh heh heh!

Get People Behind You

Give copies of the letter to all the officers of your Student Union, the editor of your student magazine, and everyone on the catering committee, and put this on the bottom of the letter. The letter should be typed, and signed by as many people as possible, including lecturers and officers of any vegetarian groups, and maybe an Indian students society.

See the President of your Student Union.

If you haven't done a petition yet, now's the time to prove just how many students want a decent choice of grub, even if they're not veggies.

The Meeting

You will probably be invited to the next Catering Committee meeting. When you arrive, remember that you have already made your case in writing. The canteen manager may be very defensive. Don't attack them or what they have been offering in the past - they probably did not know any better.

If you are unsure about avoiding deadlock arguments, we recommend you read *Getting to Yes* in the Resources chapter. For real dipsticks, er we mean intransigent people, read *Getting Past No*. Just say that the canteen should cater for all the students, and that as times are changing, you believe the menu should change too. Ask if they willing to consider vegetarian options.

Hopefully you will get an agreement to try something. If not, you have your petitions, with between 100 and 1,000 signatures, to hand to the Chair of the meeting. Remember that the Committee has the authority to tell the canteen to change. At the very least, you should get their agreement to conduct some experiments.

If you don't get what you wanted, go to the student magazine with a report of the meeting and discuss with your student union what to do next. However, this was not our experience at Bristol Polytechnic. This is what happened.

The Experiment

Although the canteen manager was clearly sceptical, Andy, one of the chefs, ate meat only twice per week. He obtained samples of vegetarian prepared meals and cloned them. He tried offering various vegetarian dishes. The nut roast was the disaster, but the five bean stew was a massive success. Meat eaters liked the new dishes too. We had to point out that on some days they offered two vegan meals, and on others nothing but veggie stuff, and he appreciated the feedback.

Getting a Result

And the result? At Bristol Polytechnic (Now the University of the West of England, Bristol or UWEB) there is now a vegetarian counter in the canteen with four dishes, of which at least one and sometimes two are vegan. They use vegetarian cheese. They still use factory farmed eggs because of cost. There is usually a bean or nut salad, but not every day. Best of all, the vegetarian counter is the most popular one of all, because loads of meat-eaters like it too!

We've done it three other times. Straightforward negotiation achieved a daily vegan dish at the canteens of British Airways and Merril Lynch, and at National Power we persuaded the cook to do extra individual dishes for vegans. Every year it gets easier. If you find you're just not getting anywhere with your canteen, write to us and we'll have a word on your behalf. We always get what we want.

Of course once you've veganized the canteen, it will make veganizing the rest of your college or workplace a whole lot easier!

How you can persuade restaurants and cafes to cater for you

Here are some things you can say or write to them.

The vegan population is growing rapidly, much faster than vegetarianism, and awareness about food allergies and cholesterol is also increasing. Therefore a very significant number of your customers will be actively avoiding eggs and dairy products as well as meat. If you make sure that many of your meals are completely animal free, you will tap into a significant market. Here are some suggestions:

1. There are numerous brands of vegetarian **sausages, burgers and bacon substitutes**. All are quite similar, but some brands contain egg. If you always buy egg-free ones, you will be able to cater for both vegetarians and vegans at the same time. For a total vegan breakfast feast, offer **scrambled** (mashed and lightly fried) **tofu** as an alternative to scrambled eggs.

2. Always have **soya milk**. It keeps for over a year unopened and up to 5 days when opened. **Soya dessert** and **soya cream** also keep for a long time. Soya milk makes excellent cappuccinos and is perfect for making custard and rice puddings.

3. Try serving **Tofutti** or **Swedish Glace** or **Provamel** ice cream, either on its own or to accompany hot pies and puddings. Just try it and you won't need any further convincing!

4. **Soya cheese** can be used to create some amazing vegan dishes, yet is rarely used in catering. It is easily available pre-packed at wholefood stores, or in bulk blocks from manufacturers and wholesalers. Redwood Foods make a very popular brand called 'Cheezley'. It has a longer shelf life than dairy cheese, even after you open it. Or make your own using

The Uncheese Cookbook by Joanne Stepaniak, from www.vrg.org or amazon.com, or ask at your bookshop.

5. Vegan salads are easy to prepare. **Egg-free mayonnaise** is available in small jars from wholefood stores or buy the excellent Plamil brand in bulk tubs from wholesalers. Alternatively make your own mayonnaise-style dressing by blending vegetable oil with roughly equal quantities of vinegar and soya milk. You could also offer a **vinaigrette** made with olive oil, herbs, mustard and lemon juice or vinegar. If you make up a big batch of this, it will keep for weeks, just shake before serving.

6. **Vegan dips** are no problem. You can easily buy or make hummous, and guacamole can be made just as well without yogurt. Try roasting aubergines and liquidising with olive oil and black pepper for a very rich and creamy baba ganoush dip.

7. For an uncooked **vegan breakfast**, serve a muesli that doesn't have honey or whey in it, or offer toast, crumpets or muffins with vegan margarine. Most brands of vegetable margarine are not vegan as they contain whey powder, but virtually all supermarkets stock at last one vegan brand. Catering size tubs can be bought from wholesalers.

8. Avoid glazing **pastries** with egg, and make sure that the pastry itself as well as the contents are vegan. Bulk packs of frozen puff, filo and shortcrust pastry are widely available from wholesalers.

9. Aim to **make at least half your starters and main courses vegan.** If only one out of four or six options is vegan we don't have any choice. Cheese, cheese or cheese isn't much of a choice for veggies either.

10. It is very frustrating that so many restaurants offer a choice of vegan starters and main courses, but no **dessert**.

When there is a dessert, it is often completely unimaginative. Vegans are as fed up with fruit salad and sorbet as vegetarians are with omelettes and cheese salad! Why not offer vegan ice cream (see above) with fruit salad, or better still, experiment with egg-free recipes for cakes and puddings. It is possible to make delicious trifles, flans and cheesecakes which are completely vegan.

If you have any questions, or would like some free vegan cake recipes, write to Ronny c/o Scamp. You could also contact the Vegan Society for their catering pack (which includes a list of wholesalers of vegan food and alcohol) and their merchandise catalogue full of cookbooks.

Alternatively, see what's on offer in any of the restaurants listed that are particularly good for vegans. The IVU and VRG websites are also a great source of inspiration.

Some good websites for recipes & cookbooks

International Vegetarian Union: www.ivu.org

The Vegetarian Society (UK): www.vegsoc.org

Vegetarian Resource Group: www.vrg.org

The Vegan Society: www.vegansociety.com

American Vegan Society, PO Box 369, Malaga, NJ 08328. Tel 856-694. Fax 856-694 2288. Fabulous catalogue of vegan cookbooks.

Food Case study

UNIVERSITY OF CALIFORNIA

Vegan students at the University of California-Berkeley are finding dorm food a little easier to swallow these days. Activists at the school have successfully petitioned for improved dorm cafeteria meals that not only skip the meat but also leave out dairy products, eggs and honey.

Berkeley has been dishing up vegetarian meals for at least seven years, says Nancy Jurich, assistant director of dining services, and vegan food had been available 90% of the time. But according to Leor Jacobi, a recent Berkeley grad and an organiser of the food reform movement, the options were inadequate. Jacobi says that vegan students had been forced to eat salad, baked potatoes and bread day in, day out.

Working with two campus groups, Students in Support of Animals and The Coalition of Students for Healthy Dorm Food, Jacobi circulated a petition for improved vegan options; he obtained signatures from 1,200 dorm residents, one fifth of all students living in dorms.

The groups then met with dorm administrators, armed with the Physician's Committee for Responsible Medicine's Gold Plan, which supplies vegan recipes and nutritional information to food service personnel, and other supportive material.

"Our seeds did fall on fertile soil," says Jacobi of Berkeley administrators, adding that Jurich, a former vegetarian, was "very open to our pleas." Following the meeting, the administrators received the results of a poll it had conducted, which showed that 15% of dorm residents are vegetarian; 5% of the total are vegan, up from 1% in 1993-94. The deal to improve vegan dorm food was sewn up at a second meeting.

On January 11th 1995, the university dining halls served an all-vegan lunch to celebrate a daily vegan menu option. About 525 people feasted on such dishes as chili, stir-fry vegetables, tofu kebabs with peanut sauce, hummus, lentil dal and rigatoni. "It went great," says Jacobi. "Only a couple of people complained about not having their meat, but we expected that."

For students who want to see more vegan - or even more vegetarian - options in the lunch line, Jacobi has a few tips: Draw attention by circulating a petition. Work with the student government; the Berkeley groups persuaded the student government to unanimously pass a resolution in support of vegan food. Have plenty of information ready to give to administrators and food service staff.

Finally, stresses Jacobi, "make sure you don't turn it into a vegetarian vs. non-vegetarian issue. Do your best to try to include everyone in the discussion."

from *Vegetarian Times*, April 1995

Vegan Action is on the Web at http://www.vegan.org

American activists are also recommended to check out the EarthSave catering pack.

chapter twelve

FUND RAISING

HOW TO GET MONEY ON STALLS WITHOUT ACTUALLY ASKING FOR IT

To do this, you **set up a single issue stall** (see chapter on this) in a shopping area. As we said in the chapter on Street Stalls, **you are not allowed to have collecting tins or ask for money on your regular stalls, but if people offer you a donation, in our experience the police won't object.**

Make sure you keep the donation column up to date on the petition. If someone doesn't give anything, put 50p or £1, then the next person will probably give the same. If you have a column of blanks you won't get anything: the first person won't give, so the next won't. However, if you put £1 on the first line, there's a good chance the next one will. If the first two do, there's an even better chance the next one will. On a full page of 25 signatures, as many as 20 could give money.

Be alert to visitors to your stall. Don't let them sign and go. The more you chat to them and give leaflets, the more likely they are to give unprompted.

Don't ever actually ask for donations or you can be prosecuted. There are subtler ways to let people know you need money. As soon as they put money on the table, get it off the table, or take their proffered shekels in your paw and stash it in a bag under the table.

If anyone asks why you don't have a tin on the table, say you've had tins stolen. If you have a basket or tin, or even just loose money on the table, that can be construed as collecting without a permit.

All donation columns should say "Optional". We've been told by the police that this is legal. If the police ask or say that you're collecting money, point out that you're not asking for it.

The optimum way to attract money is to be approachable and chatty, even bubbly.

Make some noise to attract people.

1) Bellow out what your petition's about. "End cruel animal experiments! Sign our petition."

2) Eyeball someone if you've got the guts to accept the rejections, holding your pen out, and say "Hello, would you like to sign our petition?" It works over 50% of the time.

STREET COLLECTIONS

This is where a team of you take to the street in a shopping area to collect money in cans. You cannot do this every week. **You've got to apply to the Council**. Ring up the Town Hall and ask for 'Licensing'. Fill in the form they send specifying the dates you want. The best days are Saturday or market days.

On the day, put up a stall using a wallpaper pasting table that you can get from D.I.Y stores or borrow. Unlike your regular street stall, here you can put collecting tins on the table, plus roving extras. Use as many costumes as you can get your hands on. Make sure you have posters on the stall, especially if it's a single issue stall. Some people reckon gruesome pictures get money in, others believe in cuddly ones. Try both sorts.

Each person going out with a tin could have a laminated poster on a board stuck to them so the public can see from a distance what you're collecting for. Ideally, one on the front and back, or if you're less confident stand against a wall with a board on display next to you.

Don't shake the tin too much, it annoys people. Just shake the tin a little occasionally so people know you're collecting. Anyway it's not strictly legal to shake it and we know of someone being arrested for it. The law says you should stand still, don't shake, don't shout, don't ask.

We don't like saying this but ... make sure anyone with dreadlocks hair or nose and other rings is in a costume. It does make a difference. It shouldn't but it does. We know 'cause we're quite scruffy ourselves!

Find the best spots - cover all entrances and exits to the area where you're collecting. So on a big street don't collect in the middle, set up collectors at both ends.

The most important thing to reiterate is that good visual appearance pulls in money.

Buskers can rake in money, such as when we saw five buskers on a Friends of the Earth stall with all the posters and one bod in an animal costume so that everyone could see what they were busking for.

A lot of Councils will allow you to apply for a separate licence to sell things on a stall. This **single day sales permit** is not the same as the street collection permit. So in addition you can sell T-shirts, mugs and badges. Some people sell without a licence, but you can get caught and severely dealt with.

People-friendly dogs that like to be stroked can really help, you'd be amazed how many extra donations they attract. If taking any dogs on collections, make sure they've each got a blanket to lie on and a bowl of water. Like people, they need to stretch their legs every couple of hours, so only involve dogs if this isn't a problem.

After a street collection, make sure you send the results form with the amount raised back on time and correctly filled in otherwise you'll have trouble getting a licence next time. Part of the form is to be signed by an accountant or bank manager to show that the sealed collecting tins were opened in front of them. Get yourself on a friendly rapport with a bank manager to get them to do this for free. If your manager does not want to know, then move banks.

CAR BOOT SALES AND JUMBLE

You may not think this is very glamorous, but fund raising is just as vital as campaigning. It pays for leaflets, posters and other campaign expenses. It's a good way to involve people who aren't into front-line activities like hunt sabbing or doing a demo outside a laboratory on a cold morning.

Don't allow your group to be dominated by young, radical, 'in yer face' types, when quieter, possibly older, people may be just as valuable organizing other activities which don't involve confrontation with animal abusers or hard selling our message. If someone who's not into campaigning asks what else they can do to help animals, why not ask if they are into doing jumble sales, car boots or a bring and buy coffee morning.

Collecting Tat

Type an A5 leaflet explaining all the good things your group does, concentrating on animal protection as opposed to animal rights. Say that you're collecting goods except for electrical items, which you'll get hammered for if they don't work and hurt someone. "Collecting goods (not electrical), especially books and records." Deliver it to 200 houses per night in, if possible, a relatively prosperous area, on a

Thursday or Friday night, saying that you'll be back to collect
the goods the next Thursday or Friday night. Ask that if
people are not in, that they leave the goods at the end of the
path. You could put a bin liner with each note and you'll get
loads more tat. The next week you could get 30 bags out of
the 200.

Flogging the Gear

If there are any old rags unfit to sell on a stall, you can sell to
a rag merchant in Yellow Pages, or recycle them.

Now you've got the merchandise, it's time to go to a car boot
sale. As soon as you open the boot, there'll be stacks of
people rooting through before you get it out, especially
professional car boot sale foragers. Keep your prices
reasonable. We've found small boot sales work best.
Buying animal rights merchandise to sell is not really
recommended unless you can get a good deal locally. Stuff
from "the nationals" is pricey, and you need a permit to sell it
anyway.

Jumble sales are good earners but you need loads of storage
space. Sell the average-to-poor stuff by chucking it on tables
and let people rummage. Only price up the good stuff and
sell that at car boot sales.

Alternatively at jumbles you can size up what you think a
buyer can afford. Or for simplicity everything is priced 50p
minimum and let people pay more if they want. Obviously you
won't sell a suit for 50p. Take it out and sell it at a car boot for
£5. This system is very easy to implement. Pricing up
hundreds of goods for jumbles would be a lot of work.

By the way, secondhand shops are extremely big
commitments with high overheads. The big charities nab all
the best sites, and many towns are saturated with charity
shops. So we recommend leaving these to the professionals.

It is not what they take away from you

but what you do with the rest.

chapter thirteen

THE LONG ARM OF THE LAW

PROTESTING AND THE LAW
by Tim Walker of Walkers Solicitors

INTRODUCTION

This chapter is a general introduction to the sorts of legal issues that you might encounter on a demonstration in England. It is important to note that this does not set out a comprehensive account of the law and the law is always changing. If you have any specific query then you should consult a Solicitor. If arrested, you should always speak to a Solicitor in person.

Please bear in mind that a Court may interpret the law very differently to a police officer. Police officers can be wrong about the law. Even when wrong they still have the ability to arrest you. If you are ordered to do something by a police officer and you are convinced that it is an unlawful request, you could still end up being prosecuted or being arrested if you refuse to comply.

It may also be that you are wrong in your understanding of the law. The safest way to avoid arrest is normally to comply with any direction given by a police officer.

POLICE OFFICERS

Any person attending a protest is likely to encounter police officers at some point. It is also likely that the police will give directions as to where you can and can't go, what you can and can't do and whether or not you are to be searched or to be ordered to remove face coverings. One police officer's approach to policing demonstrations may be very different to another officer's.

ARRESTABLE OFFENCES

Even if attending an entirely peaceful demonstration, it is now possible to commit a criminal offence. The most common offences people used to be arrested for were for "using threatening, abusive or insulting words or behaviour likely to cause another harassment, alarm or distress" or for "action causing a breach of the peace".

Other offences include obstructing the highway, aggravated trespass, resisting arrest and breaches of local byelaws. More recently police have been empowered to impose conditions on public assemblies ordering protestors to remain within a specific area, ordering a procession to move along a specific route and ordering a maximum amount of time for an assembly to last before it is to disband.

These provisions come under Sections 12 & 14 of the Public Order Act. If you are aware of such conditions (they are normally broadcast repeatedly over police tannoys at demonstrations and are printed on boards put up in the area of the demonstration), then you become liable to arrest and could be charged and receive a criminal conviction if you fail to comply.

Under certain circumstances police also have the power to order you to remove face coverings if they believe such coverings are worn specifically to conceal your identity.

Whenever you attend a demonstration, it is advisable to have the details of a solicitor who you can call if there are difficulties or if you are arrested.

GIVING YOUR NAME AND ADDRESS

If police stop you on a demonstration, you are not normally obliged to provide your name and address, however, if an officer suspects you of having committed an offence s/he can require you to provide your details with a view to serving a summons on you at a later date. If you refuse to provide your details under these circumstances then you can be arrested to enable the police to establish who you are so that you can be taken to court, if appropriate.

The driver of a motor vehicle can always be required to provide their name and address together with relevant driving documents.

STOP AND SEARCH

If you have not been arrested then the police can only stop and search you without your consent if the police officer has reasonable suspicion that you have in your possession goods unlawfully obtained or that you are carrying a bladed or pointed article or an offensive weapon or that you are carrying prohibited drugs. If an officer demands to search you, you should always ask what the grounds are for the search.

You are entitled to be provided with written reasons for the search after it has been undertaken. When in a public place police may only search your outer garments and you must be searched by an officer of the same sex.

In rare circumstances a senior officer can make a general authorisation for all people in a certain locality to be searched for possession of offensive weapons or dangerous instruments.

AGGRAVATED TRESPASS

Hunt saboteurs are regularly arrested for either aggravated trespass or failing to leave land when ordered to do so. You do not need to be warned that you are committing an offence in order to be arrested for aggravated trespass. If you are ordered to leave land and fail to do so as soon as practicable, then you commit an offence for which you can be arrested.

YOUR RIGHTS ON ARREST

If you are arrested then you have three rights which can only very rarely be withheld. They are:-

1. The right to consult a solicitor free of charge.

2. The right to have someone informed of your arrest.

3. The right to consult the Codes of Practice which govern your rights and what the police can and cannot do while you are in detention.

Use all three rights!

If you speak to a solicitor then you will have somebody speaking to police on your behalf to ensure that you are detained for as short a time as is possible. Furthermore, if you are going to be interviewed then you can receive advice from somebody who is committed to your interests and not the interests of any possible future prosecution.

You should always let a friend know that you have been arrested and let them know where you are. It is quite common to be released from a police station in the early hours of the morning when there are no public transport facilities available. If you have notified somebody of your arrest then they may be able to arrange for food to be brought into you and for someone to be available to collect you when you are finally released from custody.

The Codes of Practice are a small book setting out your rights while in the Police Station. You will rarely be offered anything else to read while in the cell so you might as well use your time constructively!

FOOD

If you are vegetarian or vegan then you should notify the police immediately you are booked in at the police station. This will ensure that you are not confronted by a plate of meat at mealtimes. The police should make every effort to provide you with food that you can eat, even if this involves going down to the local chippy to buy chips and beans.

YOUR CUSTODY RECORD

When you are booked into the police station, the Custody Sergeant will open a Custody Record. This details everything that takes place that relates to you whilst you are in police detention. If there is anything at all that you want to have noted about your treatment whilst you are in detention then you should ask for it to be noted on the Custody Record.

HOW LONG CAN THEY HOLD YOU

Initially the police can hold you for a maximum of 24 hours without charge. This period can be extended if you have been arrested for a serious arrestable offence.

PHOTOS, FINGERPRINTS AND DNA

In most circumstances the police do not have the power to take your photograph, fingerprints or DNA prior to charge, unless you consent. In rare circumstances police can ask a senior officer to authorise the taking of such samples to prove or disprove your involvement in a recordable offence.

If police make such a request and you are unsure of your position then you should ask to speak to a solicitor. The same applies if the police are asking if you will consent to give a blood sample or stand on an ID Parade. The police can never use force to take your photograph but in some circumstances can use force to take your fingerprints.

IF YOU ARE INJURED

If you have suffered any injuries as a result of your arrest then you should ask to be seen by the police doctor. When you are examined you should specifically state how the injuries were caused and ask the doctor to make a detailed note of all injuries. This may become relevant in any later complaint or court proceedings. Once released you should immediately ask your own doctor to examine you.

POLICE INTERVIEWS

In many circumstances the police will seek to interview you. You should always seek legal advice prior to interview and you should normally have a solicitor present during the interview. You are entitled to maintain your right to silence during interview and the police cannot force you to answer questions. However, if you do maintain your right to silence, your case goes to court and you give an account to the court then the court may choose not to believe you as you did not give this account when first questioned by police.

Maintaining your right to silence is often still advisable despite this and you should always seek legal advice as it is now such a difficult area. Remember that if you do answer police questions then you could incriminate yourself and others without realising that you are doing so.

LEGAL AID

If you are charged with a criminal offence then, except in the most minor cases, you will normally be entitled to Legal Aid, which will mean that you will not have to pay your solicitor. Your financial circumstances are no longer taken into account when the court assesses your Legal Aid Application. In rare cases you can be ordered to pay towards your defence costs but your solicitor will advise you of this beforehand.

FINAL ADVICE

Remember that it is not a foregone conclusion that you will be arrested simply because you are protesting. Many people manage to protest for years without being arrested. You will need to use your common-sense in how you behave and, at times, comply with police orders, even if you do not think they have any basis in law, if you wish to avoid arrest.

If you ever do have the misfortune to be arrested then the strongest advice is that you should say nothing whatsoever to the police other than to give your name, address and date of birth before you speak to a solicitor.

This article was written by **Tim Walker** of **Walkers Solicitors** of 2 Bouverie Road, Stoke Newington, London, N16 0AJ, Tel: 020-8800 8855, who specialise in criminal defence.

We offer a 24 hour Police Station service and preliminary free legal advice is normally available by telephone.

WALKERS

Criminal Defence Solicitors

We specialise in defending animal rights and other political activists.

We offer a 24 hour police station service and can represent you in courts throughout the Midlands and the South of England.

Call us on: 020 8800 8855

email: info@walkerssolicitors.co.uk

chapter fourteen

LET'S CHANGE THE WORLD

What is your life about?

"Search for the hero inside yourself, and then you'll find the key to your life," sings vegan Heather Small of M-People, who also appears in the video *Truth or Dairy*. We can all be heroes.

If you are touched by scenes of your favourite fictional characters saving the innocent, then you can bring that excitement, passion and caring into your everyday life. We love these stories because they touch a deep part of us that knows we are all connected in one lifestream, we are all interdependent, and we all long to rescue the pure and thwart the dark side.

Not long ago and quite nearby, a land in turmoil cried out for heroes. They were vegans, mighty activists forged in the heat of love. As long as animals and people suffered, wherever there was injustice, there would be vegan activists.

The American psychologist **Abraham Maslow** proposed that we have a hierarchy of needs. Once we've managed to take care of basic survival and shelter, we'll seek to belong to a group and to improve self-esteem. If we get this far then we can go for the pinnacle of 'self-actualisation', integrating all parts of ourselves and doing something for humanity.

In so doing we achieve our highest potential. Along the way we have 'peak experiences', experiencing the ecstacy and serenity of inner fulfilment.

Can animal rights be a path to spiritual peace and transpersonal success? We say so.

In their teens, everyone gets into some kind of "opium of the people" whether it's sport, organised religion, sex, drugs, music, computer games, work or something else.   It gets us into a group, and we enjoy the pleasure of mastering the knowledge or skills that go with group membership. All of us are chasing the delicious surge of endorphins in the brain when we belong and succeed, or simply the absence of stress.

This is fine as long as you don't surrender control of your entire life to group leaders and give up making your own decisions. Instead of turning you into a zombie, **becoming a vegan requires a healthy dose of thinking for yourself. It teaches you to stand up to coercion from people who think they have the right to tell you what to do in your own space, whether relatives, friends, priests, teachers or co-workers.**

People today feel helpless in the face of corrupt governments and giant businesses. The fact is that it just ain't so - **we are as powerful as we choose to be**. We must exercise our personal power to change those around us, and we must take political power or it will go by default to those who will abuse it.

Jacques Cousteau once recommended people to infiltrate the establishment and rise as high as they could, then use their power for good. Imagine what you might do if you woke up tomorrow and found that you were Minister for Agriculture, or Director of the Meat and Livestock Commission, or Chair of the Health Education Council, or Editor of the British Medical Journal. All these jobs and many others will be up for grabs in the future. And one day they couldl be filled by people who will do the right thing with their power and influence - people like you.

Edware Lear once asked "If it takes a cat ten minutes to kill a rat, how long does it take to kill 1,000 rats. Methinks the rats would kill the cat." It's time for us all across the world to take power and change things for the better. It may take our lifetimes, but we might be the last generation before it's too late who still have the chance to wake everyone else up. Will you join us?

Blueprint for world revolution

We have personal power to change ourselves, and by our example and provision of knowledge, those around us. When we are in the majority, (as we now are in some respects for not wearing fur, not hunting for fun, and not testing cosmetics on animals), profit-motivated big businesses eventually follow, and we can force changes in the law to mop up the last pockets of brutality. The giant cosmetics company Gillette announced at the end of 1996 the end of animal testing - as a direct result of PeTA's global campaign to wake people up, taken up by thousands of activists and millions of sympathisers. (Procter & Gamble next!)

Hunting foxes has been effectively banned by a large majority of MPs in the House of Commons as a direct result of campaigns by animal rights activists, though at the time of writing we're still waiting for Tony B'Liar to implement it. Direct protest day after day at the sites of the abuse closed down Consort, breeders of dogs for vivisection, Hillgrove cat farm, and Shamrock monkey prison, amongst others.

We can change anything we want. It's just a case of picking off the easiest targets first and moving on, building momentum for the harder targets ahead. The bad guys can't resist truth, justice, compassion and love forever.

Speak out for animals without compromise. After all, a vegan world will have huge economic benefits. Instead of speaking for less than a million meat workers, encourage MP's to speak up for six million vegetarians, sixteen million almost vegetarians, 26 million who've cut their meat consumption, 36 million whose children have been exposed to BSE by a government bribed by the meat barons, and 600 million feeling beings doomed each year by our collective insanity and inaction.

Here's a checklist of twelve things we can do to change ourselves, those who ask our help, and eventually the world, person by person and country by country. The first six are the essential stages for getting your "degree" or "black belt instructor" in veganism and animal rights, ready to deal with any situation. The other six steps are ways to use your newfound knowledge and skills to create permanent, life-saving change in others and turn all vegetarians into vegan activists.

If every vegan in the United Kingdom creates one more each year, the whole country will be safe for animals in just eight years. Why not? **Nothing is impossible unless you believe it is.**

Desk top publishing on home computers plus the Internet have for the first time in history ended the rich's monopoly on Information. There is nothing whatsoever to prevent us using our new-found power to put things right in one generation.

This book contains the knowledge you need to be part of the greatest social revolution in history, so that when you look back on your life you'll be able to think "We did something really fine. Together."

12 Steps to Change the World

1. Get the facts and go vegetarian

Send for info from Viva! and the Vegetarian Society to get you
started and use this information to become vegetarian.

2. Find out about veganism

Send some stamps to The Vegan Society for a full set of
leaflets and a catalogue. Invest in a copy of their *Vegan
Shopper*, containing everything you always wanted to know
about veganism but didn't know where to ask. Unless you're
moving towards 100% vegan, few people in the animal rights
movement will take you seriously. Get a copy of Viva's *The L-
Plate Vegan*. Read the book *Why Vegan* by Kath Clements,
available from the Vegan Society. The next two steps will take
care of any fears you may have about "coming out" as a
vegan.

3. Become a masterchef

Get a selection of vegan cookbooks. Visit local wholefood
shops, Jewish deli's and Indian, Chinese and Turkish or
Greek grocers and buy a new food every week. People don't
generally choose food because it's healthy or kind but
because it looks good and tastes nice. Become a master of
cuisine so that people are always queuing up to come to
dinner. If you come up with any really stunning creations of
your own which you would like us to publish, send them to us!

4. Learn about nutrition

Be ready for questions about calcium, protein, iron and
vitamins. Know the facts about why vegans are often the
healthiest folk on the planet. Invest in superb reference books
like *Vegan Nutrition - Pure and Simple* by Dr Michael Klaper,
Becoming Vegan by Brenda Davis and Vesando Melina, and

Vegan Nutrition by Dr Gill Langley. If funds are limited, make sure they're in your library and share books with vegetarian friends.

5. Learn about vegan babies

Often you hear people say that veganism is all very well for adults, but children need milk or meat. All complete and utter bollocks of course, but if they got it from their doctor then you'd better be ready with the truth from the real experts. Learn about vegetarian and vegan babies by sending £1.75 to Viva! for their *Mother and Baby Guide* parts 1 and 2. Learn even more about vegan children from the books *Pregnancy, Children* and the Vegan Diet by Dr Michael Klaper and *Vegan Nutrition* by Dr Gill Langley.

If your doctor tells you veganism is unhealthy for babies, give him or her these leaflets and books to read, and if that fails then change to a doctor who bothers to keep up to date. If we get all the doctors in the country to go vegan, they might just do the rest for us.

6. Learn about animal rights and ecology

Be ready to explain to pre-vegetarians the truth about animals and what we're doing to the planet. Read up on animal rights literature regularly to refresh your memory. Get extra leaflets to give out at bulk rates from the nationals. Invest in a copy of *The New Why You Don't Need Meat* by Peter Cox and *The Silent Ark* by Juliet Gellatley.

7. Become a campaigner!

Get stuck into the ideas in this book. Learn to use a word processor, write letters, give school talks, talk to the media. If you have any difficulty getting along with certain campaigners or with the public, try some of the "people" books we recommend, especially the brilliant *How to Win Friends and*

Influence People by Dale Carnegie.

8. Help your local group financially

If you're working, then give money to buy leaflets to your local groups which they can take into schools for maximum impact. Invest in the videos *Truth or Dairy* (Vegan Society), *Their Future In Your Hands* (Animal Aid), *Food For Life* (Viva!), *Animal Rights* (see inside back cover), and others from the nationals, or give them to your local school library.

9. Read campaigning magazines

Keep up to date by joining a campaigning national organisation or ten, or exchanging magazines with friends. Each of "the nationals" produces thoroughly researched materials written by the leading experts, as well as doing undercover investigations and getting the truth into the media at national level. When you've read their magazines, pass them on.

10. Tithe

If you're working and don't have much free time, you can still make things happen big time and create loads of new vegetarians by using your wages to "contract out" your campaigning. How? Consider "tithing" your income to animal rights organisations. This is the old system where people gave 10% of their income to the church. Why not start with 1% and see if you miss it? If you're single with no dependents, will you really miss £5 or £20 a month paid by standing order to an animal rights organisation?

£10 can pay for 10 packs of info that creates 10 new aware people. Every month for as long as you care to give. Or support the Vegan Society who are indundated with requests for information by people of all ages and are also very cost-effective. There are plenty of groups that will put your contribution to good use. Regular payments can be covenanted to get tax rebates, and gifts of £250 or more also get the tax back if you fill out a Gift Aid form. Don't forget to add a clause to your will.

11. Get skilled

If you're an ambitious campaigner, get tooled up for action! Contact the nationals and offer your services as a volunteer.

You can go further and take a course in journalism. Remember that the pen is mightier than the sword, but with a computer you can really kick Ronald McDonald's butt. Furthermore the Internet gives us all access to millions of people with money and information technology skills who can become campaigners, if we help them along.

12. Take and use power for truth

Get as much power as you can or influence with the the powerful (teachers, doctors, caterers, film makers, writers, politicians and the children and students who will one day be all of these) and use it to create a better world. Teach them that being a hero is about saving life.

Zen and the art of campaigning

- by Jonathon Livingston Vegan

Everything that ever was, started with a dream. Take a walk, sit or lie quietly, reflect and dream.

When you've formulated your dream, it's time to act. Success depends on action. Doing nothing is itself an action, and the most harmful one of all. It's called neglect.

Once you have taken your first steps, the path will reveal itself to you, and others will keep you company on it.

The only difference between success and failure is that success kept on going till she got there. Whatever obstacles you encounter, there are others already on the path waiting to help you in every way we can. Just ask.

You have the power to co-create a vegan world. Help others to join us on the path of truth, respect and love for all life.

We'll see you at the celebration when the last slaughterhouse closes.

Something to consider...

What goes around comes around; you get back what you give out.

It is widely believed that if you commit acts of cruelty or dishonesty, the universal law of recompense will see to it that you are shown the error of your ways, because the ultimate evolutonary pinnacle which we are all slowly moving towards is of universal love and harmony.

This principle is known as Karma. Karma can be instant, for example you insult someone and they they insult you back, or a shooter accidentally blasts themself in the leg after sending several bullets into defenceless airborne birds.

Karma can also be long-term and the effects of some actions can show up months, years or lifetimes later. Many people believe that those who cause suffering and neglect to others will one day pay the price for doing so.

Some spiritual thinkers feel that active campaigning is pointless because rather than getting stressed about injustice, we should just relax and focus on ourselves, knowing that Karma will teach the 'baddies' eventually.

However, we feel that this attitude is misguided, because if a person is aware that suffering is happening and they are in a position to do something about it, yet they choose not to, they themself are actively choosing not to help. Not helping is neglect, and neglect is an act of cruelty!

Have you ever ignored a friend in need and then felt utterly alone months or years later when you felt overwhelmed by problems? This is an example of Karma.

Whenever we say, or do, or think anything, it has global effects. Are you motivated as an activist by love or by anger?

Anger can be useful in short bursts, to motivate people to take action. However, long-term anger and resentment is usually caused by deep insecurity and it will eat away at you and can make you ill and tired. It will not make you a better campaigner.

We recommend that all campaigners learn to detach and focus. This does not mean caring less, quite the opposite.

What it means is that you can step outside of your emotional response to the suffering in the world, focus your energies and talents and then go forth and fight cruelty in a totally calm, relaxed and controlled manner.

You can feel calm inside even whilst you are in the middle of a big emotional upheaval if you learn to detach. Why not give it a try?

One technique is to recognise the moments when you are becoming very upset, frustrated or angry. Think to yourself "I am responding in a stressed way, but I am not taken over by this stress. My role at the moment is to experience this stress and use it to motivate me."

Then imagine that you are a character in a film and the events you are living through are the plot of the film. Imagine that the people whose actions are upsetting you so much are also just characters in the film, acting out their roles. Don't take their actions personally. Think about what their characters are likely to do next and write your next piece of script to act out.

Then, once you have conquered your stress, carry on with your life.

DETERMINATION

A concentrated mind achieves

more than strength alone

CHALLENGE

Always set the trail,

never follow the path

chapter fifteen

THE CAMPAIGNER'S HIT PARADE

Your DJ is Alex, who presents his personal selection of top 10 hits for activists. First up is the

CAMPAIGNER'S BOOKS TOP 10 - how to do it

1. **Campaign Against Cruelty** by us!
2. **Why Vegan** by Kath Clements
3. **The Silent Ark** by Juliet Gellatley
4. **How to Win Friends and Influence People** by Dale Carnegie
6. **Getting to Yes** by Ury and Fisher
8. **Vegan Nutrition** by Gill Langley
9. **The Vegan Shopper** by the Vegan Society
10. **Jonathon Livingston Seagull** by Richard Bach

<u>Chart tip</u> for the latest release to start storming up the charts: **Born to be Wild** by Juliet Gellatley

THE VIDEO CHART - great for talks

1. **Animal Rights** (PG) The beginner's guide to AR campaigning, see inside back cover.
2. **Food for Life** (U) Viva's introduction to vegetarianism.
3. **Their Future In Your Hands** (U) Animal Aid's intro to all the issues.
4. **Truth or Dairy** (U) Rasta supervegan Benjamin Zephaniah dishes the dirt on dairy. (Vegan Society)
5. **Food Without Fear** (U) This cracker's been in the chart longer than, er, Meat Loaf. (Vegetarian Society)

6. **Soundbites** (U) Junk, Easy, Healthy, Sporty and Gourmet Vegans' intro to cookery. (Vegan Society)

7. **For A Few Pennies More** (XXX - a real video nasty) Shocking exposé of live exports. (CIWF)

8. **McLibel** (PG) McBully gets more than he bargained for.

Red hot video tip: Animal Aid's new video, **Wasted Lives.**

THE INDIE CHART

Featuring the best independently produced books for your stalls. See the Resources section for ordering details. As we're doing the chart, we've put our own stuff in.

1. **Campaign Against Cruelty**
2. **Animal Contacts Directory** by Veggies
3. **Go Vegan** from the Vegan Society
4. **The Cake Scoffer** by Ronny
5. **The L-Plate Vegan** from Viva!
6. **Viva's baby guides** (double album)

Oi Alex, you can't put your own books in there.
It's my chart Ron. If you don't like it, do your own matey.
Right, I will then.

RONNY'S TOP TEN BOOKS FOR CAMPAIGNERS

1. **Animal Contacts Directory** by Veggies
2. **The New Why You Don't Need Meat** by Peter Cox
3. **The Vegan Shopper** by the Vegan Society
4. **The Animal Welfare Handbook** by Barry Kew
5. **Animal Rights** by Mark Gold
6. **The Cruel Deception** by Dr Robert Sharpe
7. **The Livewire Guide to Going, Being and Staying Veggie** by Juliet Gellately
8. **Peter Cox's Guide to Vegetarian Living** by Peter Cox

9. **Vegan Nutrition** by Gill Langley
10. **Why Vegan** by Kath Clements

Ronny also recommends that you read **Dogs Never Lie About Love** and **When Elephants Weep** by Jeffrey Masson and **Whale Nation** by Heathcote Williams. These books deal with the subject of animals' emotions and will remind you why you care!

VITAL VIDS

Ronny would also highly recommend the **Undercurrents** series. These are news videos professionally compiled from camcorder footage shot by activists and they are both informative, entertaining and very inspiring.

IMAGINATION

May the seeds of today

be the fruits of tomorrow

chapter sixteen

RESOURCES

This is a shopping list for tooling up for action. Check out the goodies below, select your equipment, and get out there! All prices correct at time of publication.

BRILLIANT BOOKS

Books give you the detailed story to gain the strength in depth for radio and tv discussions. When you're ready to debate with the animal abusers' public relations people, these books will furnish the facts to discredit their lies on air and give you the answers to obscure points they might raise about folic acid and mechanisms of iron absorption. Don't get angry, just get accurate and pretty soon they'll be refusing to come on if they know you'll be there.

Many books are available from **Viva!** or **the Vegan Society**. Alternatively try ordering them from bookshops or **amazon.com** (USA) or **amazon.co.uk** (UK). You will create a demand for ethical books and you'll also save the price of postage. Make sure that your group has a copy of all of them and pass them around, or persuade your local or school library to get them. We've also included some books about interpersonal skills which are just as important as knowing your subject, and you can get these from bookshops or public libraries.

TOP ANIMAL RIGHTS BOOKS

Animal Rights by Mark Gold, Jon Carpenter Publishing, £7.99. A thorough survey of all the issues, answers to the toughest questions, and heaps of practical ideas for lifestyle changes.

The Animal Welfare Handbook by Caroline Clough and Barry Kew, £9.99. An attractive looking directory of groups and what they do, plus the arguments for animal rights. A really brilliant present for a friend.

Born to be Wild by Juliet Gellatley, Livewire, £5.99. Like her earlier book *The Silent Ark*, a thorough tour of animal abuse, especially good for a young audience, plus how to fight back.

The Cruel Deception by Dr Robert Sharpe, £7.99. What's wrong with animal experiments by a PhD scientist and world authority, plus the alternatives. Thorough and easy to read.

The Dreaded Comparison by Marjorie Spiegel, £3.95. Compares human and animal slavery and will change your outlook on the world.

Fast Food Nation by Eric Schlosser, £9.99. What the all-American meal is doing to the world, with latest (2001) undercover info on how burger joint foods are really made.

Food For A Future by Jon Wynne-Tyson, £4.99. The ecology and economics of meat production and how they lead to world famine, plus the morality and history of flesh-eating.

The New Why You Don't Need Meat by Peter Cox, Bloomsbury, £4.99. Very easy to read, very thorough and good value. If you've got a friend who is curious about vegetarianism, but full of doubts, lend them this and it'll convince them how crazy meat eating is.

The Silent Ark by Juliet Gellatley, Thorsons, £6.99. Viva's founder lays bare the horrific truth about what meat farming is doing to animals and the world.

Why Vegan by Kath Clements, GMP, £6.95. The best introduction to veganism ever written, covering not just why but also how. Essential reading for all veggies.

Animal Liberation by Peter Singer. £12.50. A classic philosophical text. Powerful arguments about meat, but flawed in places as it's weak on wool and egg production.

When Elephants Weep - the emotional lives of aniamls by Jeffrey Masson, £6.99 from Animal Aid.

TOP HOW TO BE VEGGIE VOLUMES

Becoming Vegan by Brenda Davis and Vesanto Melina, Book Publishing Company, £14.99. Fantastic advice on how to actually do it by two of North America's top vegan nutritionists.

The Vegan Shopper, Vegan Society, £5.95. Lists everything you can buy that's free of animal ingredients and testing. If you're a vegan, you need this. Pocket size and handy for answering questions from pre-vegans about what to eat.

The LiveWire Guide to Going, Being and Staying Vegetarian, Juliet Gellatley, Women's Press, £3.50. Especially aimed at young women and teenagers, but great for everyone and splendid value.

Peter Cox's Guide to Vegetarian Living, Bloomsbury, £14.99. Fantastically comprehensive encyclopedia of all the issues, nutrition, health, ingredients and 300 recipes. An excellent present.

So What Do You Eat by Liz Cook, £12.95 from E. Cook, 65 Lincoln Street, Brighton BN2 2UG. Overseas pay by credit card at www.stewartdistribution.com. Gorgeous large format colourful spiral bound book with wipe-clean pages that will last forever, with lots of easy vegan recipes and heaps of information about vegan nutrition. Liz also publishes a beautiful laminated vegan nutrition chart to put on your kitchen wall for £2.95.

The Uncheese Cookbook by Joanne Stepaniak, £9.99. Make all kinds of vegan cheese at home then stick 'em on pizzas, lasagne and stacks of other calf-friendly recipes.

Vegan Nutrition by Gill Langley PhD, Vegan Society, £8.95. A summary of the scientific literature that shows that veganism is in no way less healthy than other diets. Contains a big section on babies.

Vegan Nutrition - Pure and Simple by Michael Klaper M.D., £9.95. A practical American book about veganism with all the health benefits and recipes, by the world's top vegan GP.

Don't forget to get some cookbooks, especially any with the word "vegan" in the title.

BABY TALK

Pregnancy, Children & The Vegan Diet by Michael Klaper M.D., £9.95. Nutrition, menus and all the information you need to have a vegan baby in total confidence and stand up to ignorant doctors.

Rose Elliot's Mother, Baby and Toddler Book £9.95. All you need to know about vegetarian or vegan diet before conception, pregnancy, after birth, weaning and recipes up to age two.

Vegan Infants Case Histories, £2 + 1st/2nd class stamp or international reply coupon from Plamil Foods Ltd, Folkestone, Kent CT19 6PQ. A wealth of experience of 30 vegan children from 1 to 15 years, published by the pioneers of soya infant formulas in the UK.

FOODIES

Not a Floyd, Rhodes or Naked Chef in sight, so no food that's gross, man.

Party Food for Vegetarians by Linda Majzlik, £6.99. 300 original recipes, most of which can be prepared in advance, including patés, dips, biccies, salads, cakes, desserts, summer drinks and more.
Vegan Baking by Linda Majzlik, £5
Vegan Dinner Parites by Linda Majzlik, £5

Vegan Feasts by Rose Elliot, £6.99.

The Vegan Cookbook by Alan Wakeman and Gordon Basterville, £7.99. Over 200 recipes.

Cooking for One by Leah Leneman, £8.99. New edition of *The Single Vegan*.

THE CAKE SCOFFER

by Ronny

Cheap 'n' Easy Vegan Cooking

The Cake Scoffer by Ronny, 20 pages of exciting vegan cake, dessert and sweet recipes. £1.50 for one or £2.50 for two (inc p&p), send cheque or postale order payable to S M Worsey to Scoffer Offer, PO Box 2284, London W1A 5UH. Trade prices on request.
There are tons more cookbooks from Viva!, the Vegan Society or any high street bookshop.

FAB PEOPLE BOOKS

Getting to Yes by Ury & Fisher and Getting Past No by William Ury. The best books on negotiation ever written covering the techniques of the Harvard Negotiation Project for every situation from shopping to hostages and peace treaties. The five step negotiation process involves taking a break, actively listening to the other side, making a reasonable offer and, if they walk away, leaving it on the table, developing your best alternative to negotiated agreement (BATNA) to strengthen your position, and bringing them to their senses but not their knees by giving them a taste of your BATNA. The second book covers how to deal with really difficult people.

How to Win Friends and Influence People by Dale Carnegie. The classic guide to getting along with anyone by only being positive towards them. Essential reading for all people who keep getting into verbal fights or don't think they're popular. Compulsory reading for all activists.

Making it as a Radio or TV Presenter by Peter Baker, Piatkus, £9.99. All you need to know whether you want to merely shine as a phone-in guest or one day have your own chat show.

Press Here! Managing the Media for Free Publicity, by Annie Gurton, Prentice Hall, £14.99. Ajournalist, editor and PR trainer tells you how to handle press and TV and explodes a few myths.

Surviving the Media by Diana Mather, Thorsons, £7.99. Appear successfully on TV, radio or press, by a top media expert and trainer.

INSPIRATION

Animals Diary by Mark Gold, £5. Articles, photos, recipes, campaign tips and a directory of green organisations. Available from October from Animal Aid or Jon Carpente.

Barefoot Doctor's Handbook for Heroes by Barefoot Doctor, Piatkus, £9.99. All about developing your hero qualities whilst keeping a sense of humour and protecting yourself from negativity.

Jonathon Livingston Seagull by Richard Bach. A wonderful book if you're worried about not "fitting in" with your old friends when you become a vegan or an activist.

Long Walk to Freedom, the autobiography of Nelson Mandela. The dedicated human rights campaigner tells how he and his friends liberated a nation without computers, internet or even free speech.

The Art of Happiness by the Dalai Lama & Dr Howard C. Cutler. Now we're not getting all religious on you, this is a superb book on the psychology of how to have a really great time no matter how things are going. Always find the bright side, show compassion, contribute and life is rich.

Awaken the Giant Within by Anthony Robbins. The vegan leader of a revolution in psychotherapy teaches his techniques for snapping out of apathy and building a fabulous life based on contribution.

NOVELS

Ronny likes **The Plague Dogs** by Richard Adams, and **Dr Rat** by someone we can't remember.

Alex, who's a bit of a hippy, likes **The Celestine Prophecy** and **Zen and the Art of Motorcycle Maintenance** as books that help people seize their right to think for themselves. The second one takes months to read, so keep it in the toilet. **Illusions** and **The Bridge Across Forever** by Richard Bach contain more of the same if you're into soul to soul connections and infinite love, dudes.

D-I-Y

How to Write a Vegan Book, £1.50 from Vegetarian Guides. The complete mini-guide to self-publishing a booklet such as a veggie guide to your town. Based on Alex's writing and self-publishing workshops which have resulted in many new books including the "Vegan Guide to..." series. Plus free coaching by email from Alex if you need more help. See www.vegetarianguides.com.

Print: How You Can Do It Yourself! by Jonathon Zeitlyn, Journeyman Press. A simple, step-by-step guide for people who want to print their own posters, leaflets or even books.

ADVANCED PEOPLE BOOKS

If you find yourself in the position of coordinating a group or chairing meetings, you will run across a range of people who will try to make your life difficult. There'a a whole literature about antisocial behaviour aimed at psychologists and therapists, much of which is filtering down to the lay level. Most of it comes from America so check out amazon.com if you can't find them locally.

Some of the behaviours you'll need to be able to recognise include passive aggression; the different levels of human conversations in terms of Parent, Adult and Child modes; and of course subtle and blatant intimidation or bullying. Good introductory texts are

Games People Play by Dr Eric Berne.

I'm OK You're OK by Thomas A Harris. An introduction to transactional analysis.

Bullying at Work by Andrea Adams. Includes the psychology of bullies, who actually fear you.

How to Deal with Difficult People by Ursula Markham.

Dealing With People You Can't Stand - How to Bring Out the Best in People at Their Worst, by Dr Rick Brinkman & Dr Rick Kirschner. Survive and possibly thrive with personalities like the Tank, the Sniper, the Know-It-All, the Think-They-Know-It-All and the Whiner. We've all had our lives made miserable by them, but they may see us as one of these types till we understand what's really going on.

The Golden Rules of Advocacy by Keith Evans. A top barrister explains how to get liars to dig themselves a hole by using quiet questions rather than accusatory statements. Invaluable for exposing someone pulling the wool over your colleagues' eyes.

Never Be Lied To Again by David J. Lieberman. As used to train police forces. Spot the weasels and also discover the barrage of techniques police interrogators use to trick confessions out of people they have no proof against who didn't keep their mouths shut.

And finally some really advanced books:

The Art of Strategy by Sun Tzu, the translation by R L Wing. The unwritten rules of intra- or inter-organizational warfare. "The highest skill is not to win one hundred victories in one hundred battles, but to subdue the enemy without fighting."

Territorial Games - Understanding and Ending Turf Wars at Work, by Annette Simmons. If you have one person or clique dominating a group and sabotaging forward progress, understand what really drives them and how to unblock the organization.

The Magic of Conflict by Tomas F. Crum. A wonderful book to keep you smiling while having fun dealing with the above.

STUFF FOR STALLS

BOOKS IN BULK

Scamp, PO Box 2284, London W1A 5UH. For ordering bulk copies of this book and *The Cake Scoffer* cookbook.

Jon Carpenter Publishing, The Spendlove Centre, Charlbury, Oxfordshire OX7 3PQ. Tel 01608-811969, Fax 01608-811969. Catalogue of books and booklets, some as cheap as 50p, which are brilliant for selling on stalls. 20% discount on orders over £20 (retail), 35% over £35, post free. Send for their latest catalogue.

BUSTIN' BOOKLETS

The following 3 booklets are available from ARC News, PO Box 339, Wolverhampton WV10 7BZ. Cash, postal order or cheque to ARC News.

Consuming the Planet The eco-politics of veganism. Sample copy free for an A5 SAE. Write for details of bulk orders to ARCnews.

A Beginner's guide to Animal Rights by Ronny. The basic principles. 50p per copy. Bulk (10+) copies for 30p each.

Betrayed by ARCnews. Excellent booklet of hard-hitting photos. Same price as above.

LUSCIOUS LEAFLETS

Leaflets are cheap. This is just a selection and there are loads more from all the national campaigning groups. We suggest you get all of them for reference. Usually you can obtain one of each leaflet free by sending a couple of stamps.

Leaflets from the nationals have been thoroughly researched and you can count on them to be accurate and up to date. They look good, are cheap in bulk, and save a lot of explaining. They've been clearly written by journalists and advertising experts to have maximum impact and inspire people to act at once.

However beware of some leaflets that are basically a big advertisement for a national, along the lines of "Send us £20 and we'll sort it out." The charities that only campaign for "fluffy" animals like elephants, cats and dogs are notorious for this. Go for the leaflets that tell people what they can do themselves to create change today by making lifestyle changes. Or use the information in them as the basis for your own leaflets.

Milk, Health, Leather, Ecology Four leaflets from the Vegan Society, available in bulk.

The Vegan Society's catalogue of books and other goodies.

Animal Aid have a wide and constantly expanding range of excellent colour leaflets covering subjects such as vivisection, factory farming and vegan cooking.

Animal Aid's *merchandise catalogue* including shampoo and conditioner and the *Living Without Cruelty* diary.

BUAV produce A5 leaflets about animal testing and experiments.

CAPS have leaflets which dish the dirt on zoos.

CAFT produce anti-fur leaflets, as do **CALF**

Campaign for the Abolition of Angling do anti-fishing leaflets for adults and children, along with stickers and t-shirts.

Compassion in World Farming (CIWF) produce colour leaflets on factory farming, battery cages and live exports.

Ethical Wares colour catalogue is full of shoes and boots and now other vegan products.

NAVS produce leaflets on dissection and violence free science. **Animals Defenders** leaflets about circuses, chicken farming, bullfighting are also available through NAVS.

PeTA have stacks of leaflets, stickers and information sheets.

Respect for Animals produce a leaflet about the fur trade. Free for small quantities.

Vegetarian Shoes colour catalogue. Great for giving to people who want to go totally vegan.

Veggies has a variety of leaflets and posters, plus the *Animal Rights Calendar*, which you can order in bulk and give away.

What's Wrong With McDonald's leaflets available for £12 per 1000 from Veggies. There's also a giant leaflet which will cost a lot to give away but is essential reading. You can send less money and they'll send you less leaflets.

Go Veggie with Paul McCartney from Viva! A giant 8-page leaflet covering the basics of why you should be a veggie, aimed especially at teenagers but good for everyone.

Viva's merchandise catalogue containing some particularly groovy T-shirts. A bulk order form is available for local groups affiliated to Viva! which lists their leaflets, stickers, badges etc. They also produce a set of bargain booklets you can read in half an hour each or less covering all the basic areas including nutrition, BSE, health, recipes, animal rights, environment and veganism.

Books for Life Viva's catalogue containing lots of answers to the question "What would you like for your birthday?"

Viva! have also published **Rose Elliot's Mother and Baby Guide**, part one on pregnancy, part two on feeding. Both are written from a vegan viewpoint demolishing the myth that cow's milk is good for babies.

Viva's **The L-Plate Vegetarian** and **The L-Plate Vegan** are crammed with ideas for new vegetarians and vegans. The first one uses a fair bit of egg and dairy for new veggies, but also gives loads of info on the vegan versions made from tofu or soya. Groups affiliated to Viva! can order in bulk.

The Vegetarian Society are now producing vegan recipe leaflets.

National and local organisations are continually updating their leaflets. We suggest you write to them all for their latest list with a stamped self-addressed envelope.

CAMPAIGNS KIT

MANUALS AND REPORTS

Animals Contacts Directory published by Veggies, £4.95. Huge directory of every animal rights group, animal sanctuary, vegetarian and vegan business in the UK, plus hundreds of overseas contacts.

Animal Rights Calendar £4 per year from Veggies. List all demos and national meetings for the next few months. These are great places to meet other activists, share techniques and materials and make new friends. Alternatively consult their website.

The Extended Circle by Jon Wynne-Tyson, £7.50. Anthology of famous people's views on animal righs, full of quotes and rerences to tool you up for writing and debates.

A Guide to Speaking in Schools from the Vegetarian Society.

How To Win Debates With Vivisectionists booklet by Dr Vernon Coleman, who regularly trashes top scientific fraudsters on TV. £1.50 from Plan 2000.

The Silence of the Lambs Animal Aid's report on the scandal of sheep meat and wool.

The Viva! Guide to Speaking in Schools Packed with ideas on

how to give the talk and answers to all the most common questions.
Send £2.50 to cover the cost of copying and postage.

Vegan Society Catering Pack £1.95. As used by Alex to get daily
vegan meals introduced in the canteens at Bristol Poly, British
Airways, National Power, Merrill Lynch etc. It works!

VivaCity! Viva's newsletter for local campaigning groups.

VITAL VIDEOS

All the nationals produce videos that you can use in talks. This is a
selection of popular ones for a general talk on animal rights,
vegetarianism or veganism.

Animal Rights. Introduction to animal rights and campaigning, with
undercover footage of all kinds of animal abuse, interviews with
successful activists, the psychology of change and first steps to
activism. See inside back cover.

Devour the Earth. The Vegetarian Society, 20 minutes. Paul
McCartney explains how animal farming is destroying the planet.

Food for Life. Viva's new schools vegetarian video covering animal
rights and nutrition. 24 mins. Unfortunately not entirely vegan.

Food Without Fear. The Vegetarian Society. 20 minute video made
especially for school talks.

For A Few Pennies More. CIWF. Shocking footage of the live
export trade. A good one to show before going on a demo.

McLibel Video Dave and Helen tell why they fought the longest libel
trial ever in Britain. Exposes what McDonald's do to animals and the
planet and makes a stand against corporate intimidation.

Sad Eyes and Empty Lives Powerful anti-zoo footage from CAPS.

Pisces Video. (from CAA) Shows how angling, the neglected
bloodsport, also kills other wildlife with the deadly tackle left behind.
£6, or hire for £6 including £5 returnable deposit.

Soundbites. The Vegan Society's 30 minute cookery video from junk to gourmet.

Their Future In Your Hands. Animal Aid, 11 minutes. Covers all areas of animal rights and perfect for showing at the start of a (school) talk. This video has been dubbed into many languages.

Truth or Dairy The Vegan Society, £9. 20 minutes of pure joy as vegan celebrities tell us why they ditched dairy, eggs and leather. Funny and brilliant for talks and showing to all your friends.

Wasted Lives: The Case against Animal Experiments. 20 mins, Animal Aid. £5 inc p&p, comes with teachers' notes. 2 versions, one for adults and 6th form and a milder one for younger folk.

MAGAZINES

Animal Times. Colour magazine of PETA. Excellent coverage of high profile protests throughout Europe and America. Loaded with ideas for local campaigns. You have to join PETA to receive it, but they'll happily send you a sample copy.

ARCNews. The monthly mag of the Animal Rights Coalition. £10 per year, 11 monthly issues. News for local animal rights campaigners in the UK with a full diary of upcoming AR events. ArcNews, PO Box 339, Wolverhampton WV10 7BZ. Tel 0845 458 0146. email: james@arcnews.demon.co.uk. http://www.envirolink.org/arrs/arc/

Arkangel, BCM 9240, London WC1N 3XX. Available through subscription for £10 (4 issues) or £2 (sample). The animal liberation magazine with a wholly positive approach. Contains a massive directory of local and national animal rights groups, sabbing news, lists of sanctuaries, news from the ALF Press Office, latest successes and an open forum for debate. Beautifully illustrated.

NAHC Newsletter. Very good. Packed with news and info on various anti-bloodsports campaigns and merchandise list. National Anti Hunt Campaign, PO Box 66, Stevenage, Herts SG1 2TR.

Outrage. Magazine of Animal Aid with latest information on national campaigns that your group can take up.

London Animal Rights News Packed with news. £5 (waged) or £3 (unwaged) per year to LAA, BM Box 2248, London WC1N 3XX. Tel/fax 0845-458 4775. www.londonaa.demon.co.uk

Pisces Anti-angling newsletter with details of what you can do to fight the most widespread bloodsport. Available from CAA.

The Vegan Quarterly magazine of the Vegan Society. £1.95 per issue.

Vegan Views magazine, 6 Hayes Ave, Bournemouth BH7 7AD. £4 p.a. or one copy £1, Europe & surface £5, airmail outside Europe £7.

The Vegetarian Magazine of the Vegetarian Society. Campaign news and listings of places to eat, shop and holiday.

VegNews North America's new national vegan newspaper. $20 for 10 issues per year in North America or $40 overseas. See www.vegnews.com. Also available in Europe via Vegetarian Guides.

Vivactive Viva's campaigning newsletters for U-18's.

VivaLife Campaigning newsletter for everyone.

Wildlife Guardian Newspaper of the League Against Cruel Sports.

THE UK NATIONALS

Do you know your LACS from your HSA? Veggies from VegSoc? Write to them all with a couple of stamps for their catalogues of campaigning materials. Never, ever, write to them without enclosing at least a stamp. Remember, these are charities and most of them are unable to do as much as they'd like because of shortage of dosh. Don't abuse them.

ALF Supporters Group, BCM Box 1160, London WC1N 3XX. Subscription £24 or £2 per month. Leaflets, posters, mugs, T-shirts. Selling any of these perfectly legal items openly no stalls will probably get you banned in some places like schools but attract lots of interest in others, such as at free festivals. The ALF has a clear policy of non-violence and no person or animal has ever been harmed by an ALF action. (Compare this to the unlawful killings of Jill Phipps, Tom Worby and Mike Hill, hospitalization of many hunt sabs, and the hundreds killed every week by government promoted animal products)

The SG magazine does report the potentially violent actions against professional animal abusers of other groups such as the Animal Rights Militia or Justice Department, but clearly states that it is against attacks on people, no matter how misguided or just plain evil they are. They raise funds to help pay fines and to pay towards the travelling expenses of relatives making prison visits.

Funds also pay for books, cruelty-free toiletries and other needs of animal rights prisoners. One day people who rescue animals from prison won't end up there themselves, and those who abuse and kill animals or beat up peaceful protestors, will. Until then, the SG supports those imprisoned for saving animals' lives.

Animal Aid The Old Chapel, Bradford St, Tonbridge, Kent TN9 1AW. Tel 01732-364546. Fax 366533. £12 waged, £8 unwaged, £5 youth. The experts on U-18 campaigns for all areas of animal rights including vivisection, school dissection, school debates, displays, veganism, circuses. Excellent leaflets, Recipe for Life guide for new veggies, video Their Future In Your Hands, Humane Research Donor Card. Huge network of local and youth groups. Newsletter Outrage. Organises annual Take the Veggie Pledge month.

Born Free Foundation 3 Grove House, Foundry Lane, Horsham, West Sussex RH13 5PL. Tel 01403-240170, Fax 01403-327838. Projects include Zoo Check, Elefriends, Into The Blue, Operation Wolf, Great Ape Escape.

British Anti-Vivisection Association (BAVA), PO Box 82, Kingswood, Bristol BS15 1YF. Campaigns against vivisection not on ethical grounds but only as medical and scientific fraud, based on the books Slaughter of the Innocent and Naked Empress by Hans Ruesch. You should know that some of their supporters (who probably haven't read our 'people' books) believe other organizations are in the pockets of the vivisectors, and they can get very angry with you if you express a different view!

BSE Helpline 01273-777688. Latest advice on BSE/CJD from scientific consultants, nutritionists and dieticians. Operated by Viva!

British Union for the Abolition of Vivisection (BUAV), 16a Crane Grove, Islington, London N7 8LB. Tel 020 7700 4888 Fax 7700 0252. Against all animal experiments. Lots of superb posters for your stalls including cats, dogs and monkeys in labs. Publishes reports and factsheets.

Campaign for the Abolition of Angling BM FISH, London, WC1N 3XX. Tel 020-7278 3068. Newsletters, factsheets, video, Anti-Angling week in June, protests outside fishing shops, sabbing anglers and persuades businesses to stop sponsoring matches. Provides speakers for talks and public meetings. Formerly Pisces.

Campaign Against the Fur Trade (CAFT) Po Box 38, Manchester, M60 1NX.

Campaign Against Leather & Fur (CALF), BM 8889, London WC1N 3XX. Factsheets on leather, wool, silk, exotic animal skins.

Captive Animals Protection Society (CAPS) PO Box 43, Dudley, West Midlands DY3 3YP, Tel 01384-456682, Fax 01384 456682. Exposes the suffering of animal circuses, lobbies councils to ban animal acts & educates the public.

Compassion in World Farming (CIWF), 5a Charles St, Petersfield, Hampshire GU32 3EH. Tel 01730-264208 or 268863. Fax 01730-260791. £14, unwaged £6. Campaigns against factory farming and live exports. Leaflets, posters, hard-hitting videos, national demos and lobbies of Parliament.

Dr Hadwen Trust 84a Tilehouse St, Hitchin, Herts, SG5 2DY. 01462 436 819. Info about animal-free research, plus they stock the best range of vegan chocolates available anywhere!

Environmental Investigation Agency (EIA) 15 Bowling Green Lane, London EC1R 0BD. Tel 020-7490 7040, Press 020-7490 7046, Fax 020-7490 0436. Research, investigation, campaigns, Pilot whaling, trade in ivory, pets and other endangered species.

Hunt Saboteurs Association (HSA), PO Box 2786, Brighton BN2 2AX. Tel 01273 622 827. Can put you in touch with your local sabbing group. Leaflets, posters, videos and legal advice.

International Fund for Animal Welfare (IFAW) 8th Floor, 87-90 Albert Embankment, London SE1 7UD. Tel 020-7587 6700, Fax 020-7587 6720. info@ifaw.org. www.ifaw.org. Worldwide campaigns against all abuse of animals and their environment.

League Against Cruel Sports (LACS), Sparling House, 83-87 Union Street, London SE1 1SG. Tel 0171-403 6155 or 407 0979. £12 sub. Sales catalogue, anti-hunting and shooting leaflets, posters, videos. Working for the end of recreations which involve killing animals for pleasure. Publishes Wildlife Guardian.

McLibel Support Campaign, c/o 5 Caledonian Rd, London N1 9DX. Tel 020-7713 1269. Fax 7713 1269. Support for defendants who resisted libel action for telling the truth about McMurderers.

Movement for Compassionate Living, 31 Florence Ave, Maidenhead, Berks, SL6 8SJ. Information on veganism, especially using trees to grow food. Publishes Abundant Living in the Coming Age of the Tree, £1.80.

National Anti Hunt Campaign, PO Box 66, Stevenage, Herts SG1 2TR. Independent anti hunting group.

National Anti-Vivisection Society (NAVS), 261 Goldhawk Rd, London W12 9PE. Tel 020-8846 9777. Fax 8846 9712. Campaigns for violence-free science in education, undercover investigations in labs, TV documentaries. Leaflets, posters, videos. Publishes *Campaigner* and *Animals Defender*. Membership £17, £9.50 (unwaged).

PeTA Europe (People for the Ethical Treatment of Animals), PO Box 3169, London SW18 4WJ. Tel 020-8870 3966. High-profile campaigns including vivisection, fur, veganism. Huge range of factsheets on all areas of animal rights. Free info packs on various issues. Leaflets, posters, stickers, badges. Excellent books *Save the Animals* and *Free the Animals*.

Plan 2000, 234 Summergangs Rd, Hull HU8 8LL. Tel 01482-786855. Set up by journalist, writer and former GP Dr Vernon Coleman to end vivisection. Merchandise list includes videos and the booklet *How to Win Debates With Vivisectionists*.

Respect for Animals, PO Box 500, Nottingham NG1 3AS. Tel 0115-952 5440, Fax 0115 979 9159. Campaigns against fur. Membership £15, or £7.50 (unwaged).

RSPCA Linkline Lo-call 0990-555999. Confidential national phone line to pass on information about cruelty to animals.

Save the Newchurch Guinea Pigs, PO Box 74, Evesham, Worcs, WR11 5WF. Campaigning to close down a huge breeder of animals for vivisection. Tel 01902 564 734. email info@guineapigs.org.uk

Stop Huntingdon Animal Cruelty (SHAC), PO Box 381, Cheltenham, Glos, GL50 1YN. High profile campaigns against Huntingdon Life Sciences. See their ad for details. www.shac.net Tel 0121-632 6460

Uncaged, 14 Ridgeway Road, Sheffield S12 2SS. Tel 0114 253 0020 fax 0114-265 4070. National boycott of Procter and Gamble for testing household products on animals, demos. Membership £12 or £6 (unwaged).

Vegan Prisoners Support Group, PO Box 194, Enfield, EN1 3HD. 020 8292 8325 email hvpc@vpsg.freeserve.co.uk Gives moral support to AR prisoners. Works with the prisoner through the prison authority to obtain a proper nutritional vegan diet, vegan toiletries etc. Tries to make their incarceration more bearable by providing advice and support wherever possible, giving them a lifeline and contact number.

The Vegan Society, Donald Watson House, 7 Battle Rd, St Leonards-on-Sea, East Sussex TN37 7AA. Tel 01424-427393, Fax 717064. Membership £17 or £11 (unwaged). Leaflets on milk, health, leather, environment. Publishes *The Vegan* magazine, *The Vegan Shopper*, *Vegan Nutrition* and the video *Truth or Dairy*. Merchandise catalogue. Network of local contacts and individuals campaigning for veganism.

The Vegetarian Society (VSUK), Parkdale, Dunham, Altrincham, Cheshire WA14 4QG. Tel 0161-928 0793. Fax 0161-926 9182. £21 (£16 unwaged, £8 U-16) brings you four copies of *The Vegetarian*. Leaflets, merchandise, posters and a huge network of local groups and contacts. You can get posters and leaflets for National

Vegetarian Week in June, but some of their recipes contain eggs and dairy, making them unacceptable to most campaigners.

Veggies, 245 Gladstone St, Nottingham, NG7 6HX. Tel 0845 458 9595. Catalogue of low priced leaflets, posters, McLibel stuff. Publishes the *Animal Rights Calendar* (£4 per year) and *Animal Contacts Directory* (£4.95). Caterers to the animal rights movement.

Viva! (Vegetarians International Voice for Animals), 12 Queen's Square, Brighton BN1 3FD. Tel 01273-777688, Fax 776755. £12 waged, £9 unwaged, £4.99 U-18. Runs training courses for school speakers. Literature and merchandise, book catalogue, stickers, badges, posters, T-shirts, guides to going veggie and vegan. Network of local contacts and school speakers.

WORLD WIDE WEB SITES

Animal Rights Resource Site www.envirolink.org/arrs/ has a menu leading to vegan sites like /PETA and /arc (for ARCNEWS).

Mad Cow Disease Home Page www.mad-cow.org/
Info concerning BSE for the scientific world www.airtime.co.uk/bse/

RCS Cheap printing of colour leaflets & booklets www.rcs.plc.uk (For black and white leaflets: **Good Time Print**, Sabah House, Harbourne Lane, High Halden, Kent TN26 3JF. Tel 01233-850712. Fax 01233-850869.)

ROXY

National Animal Rights Groups

Animal Aid   http://www.animalaid.org.uk/

Animal Rights Coalition   http://arc.enviroweb.org/

Born Free Foundation   http:// www.bornfree.org.uk.

BUAV   http://www.buav.org/

CAA   http://www.anti-angling.com/

CAPS http://www.caps-uk.dircon.co.uk/

EIA   http://www.eia-international.org.

Hunt Saboteurs Association http://www.huntsabs.org.uk/

IFAW   http://www.ifaw.org.

League Against Cruel Sports http://www.league.uk.com/

National Anti Vivisection Society http://www.navs.org.uk/

PeTA   http://www.peta-online.org/

Respect for Animals   http://www.respectforanimals.org/

Save the Newchurch Guineapigs   http://www.guineapigs.org.uk

Stop Huntingdon Animal Cruelty http://www.shac.net

Uncaged   http://www.uncaged.co.uk/

Veggies   http://www.veggies.org

Viva!   http://www.viva.org.uk/

**To find any local or national group or sanctuary, use the Animal Contacts Directory
http://www.veggies.org.uk/acd/index.htm**

For groups worldwide, use World Animal Net
http://www.worldanimal.net/

Information about vegan nutrition, practical advice etc.

Mother and Baby guide
http://www.viva.org.uk/Viva!Guides/baby1.html

Physicians Committee for Responsible Medicine (PCRM)
www.pcrm.org. 5,000 doctors promoting vegan food.

Vegan ecology and health by the author of *Diet for a New America*
www.earthsave.org/

Vegan PhD nutritionist Mark Messina's of PCRM detailed site
www.olympus.net/messina/

Vegan Society homepage http://www.vegansociety.com/

Vegan Society Info sheets
http://www.vegansociety.com/info/infohome.html

Vegetarian Resource Group http://www.vrg.org/index.htm

Vegetarian Society http://www.vegsoc.org/

Vegsource (discussion boards) http://www.vegsource.com/

Ethical Shopping

Animal Friends Insurance   http://www.animalfriends.org.uk/

Duck Direct (cheap bulk vegan food)
http://www.duckdirect.com/Food.asp

Ethical Wares (shoes, belts) http://www.ethicalwares.com/

Honesty (entirely vegan cosmetics)

http://freespace.virgin.net/honesty.cosmetics/

Veganline (leather-look shoes)
http://www.musonix.demon.co.uk/veganline/

Veganstore (food, shoes etc.) http://www.veganstore.co.uk/

Vegan Village (lots of links) http://www.veganvillage.co.uk/

Vegetarian Shoes   http://www.vegetarian-shoes.co.uk

Other Useful Sites

This Book http://www.campaignagainstcruelty.co.uk/

Scamp http://www.scampsite.co.uk

Animal Ingredients A-Z   http://animal-ingredients.hypermart.net/

Jeffrey Masson (animal rights writer) http://www.jeffreymasson.com/

Land and Liberty (vegan permaculture info)
http://pages.unisonfree.net/gburnett/landlib/

McSpotlight http//www.mcspotlight.org/ An on-line interactive
library of everything McDonald's don't want the public to know,
making full use of text, graphics, video and audio.

Movement for Compassionate Living
http://pages.unisonfree.net/mcl/

No Whey Campaign
http://www.veganconsumer.uklinux.net/nowhey.shtml

Vegan Central (up to date news roundup)
http://www.vegancentral.com/vc/

Vegan Village Food Links page
http://www.veganvillage.co.uk/fddrnk.htm

Networking and Moral Support

Vegan Family House (advice and support)
http://www.veganfamily.co.uk/

Vegsource (discussion boards, based USA)
http://www.vegsource.com/

Vegan Community Support (lots of links)
http://www.iptoolz.com/vegan-net/new

Young Vegan Network (a new club 18-30)
http://groups.yahoo.com/group/vegan-network

A SUMMARY OF UK NATIONAL GROUPS

Here is a list of animal rights topics and the national groups which
can provide information about them.

ANIMAL EXPERIMENTS
Animal Aid, British Union for the Abolition of Vivisection, British Anti
Vivisection Association, National Anti Vivisection Society, PETA, Plan
2000, Save the Newchurch Guineapigs, SHAC, Uncaged.

BLOODSPORTS
Campaign for the Abolition of Angling, Hunt Saboteurs Association,
League Against Cruel Sports, National Anti Hunt Campaign, RSPCA.

DIET/ ANIMAL FARMING
Animal Aid, Compassion In World Farming, McLibel, PETA, Vegan
Society, Vegetarian Society, Veggies, Viva!

ANIMAL SKINS
Campaign Against Leather and Fur, Respect for Animals, PETA,
Vegan Society.

WILDLIFE / ZOOS
Born Free Foundation, Captive Animals Protection Society,
Environmental Investigation Agency, IFAW.

Australian Groups

Vegans International(Australia)
Elizabeth Wolf, PO Box 1215, Lismore, NSW 2480
ph 61(2)6689 7461
email vegansofvia@lis.net.au   veganwolf@hotmail.com

The Vegan Society (NSW)
Luis Rappaport, PO Box 467, Broadway, NSW 2027
ph 61(2)9904 6789
email aura@zip.com.au   http://www.vegansociety.com

The Vegan/Vegetarian Society(QLD)
1086 Waterworks Road, The Gap, QLD 4061
ph/fax 61(7)3300 1274

The Vegan Society (SA) and the Ethical Treatment of Animals
George Karolyi, PO Box 84, Upper Sturt, Adelaide, SA 5156
ph 61(8)8370 8539

All members of the societies below recieve *New Vegetarian and Natural Health* magazine quarterly as part of their membership.

The Vegetarian Society (NSW)
Mark Berriman, PO Box 65, Paddington, NSW 2021
ph 61(2)9698 4339 fax 61(2)9310 5365
email:avs@moreinfo.com.au

The Vegetarian Society(ACT)
Jyoti Dambiec, ph 61(2)6258 6632
email:dambiec@ozemail.com.ao http://www.vegact.findhere.com

The Vegetarian Society(NTH QLD)
Wayne Roy, ph 61(7)4723 1122

The Vegetarian Society (WA)
Robert Fraser, ph 61(8)9474 2172 email:vswa@ivu.org

The Vegetarian Society (SA)
Mick Fernside, ph 61(8)8261 3194

Vegetarian Network Victoria
Richard Dimech, ph 61(3)9415 7166

Animal Rights and Rescue
Barbara Stefferson, PO Box 16, Wollongbar, NSW 2477
ph 61(2)6628 1358, fax 61(2)6628 7398
Companion Rescue and rehome -NO KILL

Animal Liberation Newcastle
Mark Pearson, PO Bo 136, Newcastle, NSW 2300
ph 61(2)4952 4121, fax 61(2)4957 7342
Affiliated with Animal Lib NSW and promotes ACTION MAGAZINE

Animal Liberation (NTH NSW)
Karen Bevis and Chris Simcox, PO Box 477, Lismore
NSW 2480
ph 61(2)6688 6119, email: karen@wild.net au

International Network for Animals and Religion
Alice Shore, PO Box 86, Birdwood, SA 5234

American Groups

People for the Ethical Treatment of Animals (PETA)
501 Front St. Norfolk, VA 23510
Tel.: 757-622-7382, Fax: 757-622-0457
peta@peta-online.org, www.peta-online.org
The largest animal rights organization in the world.

Physicians Committee for Responsible Medicine (PCRM)
P.O. Box 6322, Washington, DC 20015
Tel.: 202-686-2210, Fax: 202-686-2216
www.pcrm.org, pcrm@pcrm.org
Comprised of physicians and lay members; promotes nutrition,
preventative medicine, and ethical research practices.

Fund for Animals
World Building, 8121 Georgia Ave., Suite 301, Silver Spring, MD
20910-4933
Tel.: 301-585-2591, Fax: 301-585-2595
hdquarters@fund.org, www.fund.org
Specializes in hunting issues and other animal protection issues.

The Humane Society of the United States (HSUS)
2100 L St. NW, Washington, DC 20032
Tel.: 202-452-1100, Fax: 202-778-6132
www.hsus.org, E-mail from: http://www.hsus.org/forms/contact.html
Focuses on campaigns such as fur, companion animals, and humane
treatment of farm animals.

The American Anti-Vivisection Society
801 Old York Rd., #204, Jenkintown, PA 19046
Tel.: 215-887-0816, Fax: 215-887-2088, www.aavs.org
Deals with animal experimentation issues.

American Vegan Society
P.O. Box H, Malaga, NJ 08328
Tel.: 609-694-2887
Has an extensive list of available vegetarian books and sponsors
annual conferences.

Animals' Agenda
P.O. Box25881, Baltimore, MD 21224
Tel.: 410-675-4560, www.animalsagenda.org
A comprehensive animal rights bi-monthly magazine.

Last Chance for Animals
8033 Sunset Boulevard, Suite 35, Los Angeles, CA 90046
Tel.: 310-271-1890 or 1-888-88-ANIMAL, Fax: 310-271-1890

Vegetarian Resource Group
P.O. Box 1463, Baltimore, MD 21203
Tel.: 410-366-8343, Fax: 410-366-8804, www.vrg.org
Dedicated to health, ecology, ethics, and world hunger education;
produces and sells books and pamphlets.

VegNews
PO Box 2129, Santa Cruz, CA 95063-2129
Tel: 408-358 6478, Fax: 408-358 7638
Finally, since July 2000 our movement is united by a national
monthly newspaper of veganism and animal rights, home and
foreign travel, campaigns, food, reviews, interviews with activists,
events, listings, sheer inspiration. Subscription $20 in US, $30
Canada, $40 worldwide. www.vegnews.com

Other helpful resource sites:

animalconcerns.netforchange.com: This Web site provides up to
date information about events, animal issues, and locating other
groups and activists.

http://www.animalrights2001.org
Massive USA annual summer activist training and planning gathering
organised by Farm Animal Reform Movement, just increment the
year for future events and check out past ones.

http://www.circuses.com

http://www.cowsarecool.com/

http://www.milksucks.com

htttp://www.notmilk.com

PeTA's bookshop, http://www.peta.org/pm/books/index.html

http://www.virunga.org/ Animal protection (mainly wildlife)

How it all Vegan (cookery) http://www.govegan.net/

Vegan Action http://www.vegan.org/

Vegan Outreach http://www.veganoutreach.com

Vegetarian and Vegan Baby and Child
http://www.vegetarianbaby.com/

There are those that sit and talk

about what they dream of doing

and others who go out

and do something about it.

SWEDISH GROUPS

Animal Rights Sweden

Box 2005
S-125 02 Älvsjö
(visitor address: Gamla Huddingevägen 437)
Tel: +46-8-555 914 00
Fax: +46-8-555 914 50
email: info@djurensratt.org
Website: www.djurensratt.org
Magazine: Djurens Rätt (Animal Rights) five times a year

Sweden's biggest animal rights organisation with 50,000 members, founded in 1882, previously called the Swedish Society Against Painful Experiments on Animals. They run campaigns throughout the year including International Animal Day and Fur Free Friday. Main areas of concern are alternatives to animal testing, cosmetics not tested on animals, improving the situation of farm animals, banning of battery cages, stopping keeping animals for fur production, veganism and vegetarianism. The main reason for changing its name was to show that the society deals with all kinds of animal rights issues, cooperating internationally with WSPA, IAAPEA, The European Coalition to End Animal Experiments and Eurogroup for Animal Welfare.

Swedish Vegan Society

Klövervägen 6
647 30 Mariefred
Tel/Fax: +46-159-344 04
email: u.troeng@strangnas.mail.telia.com
Magazine: Vegan four times a year.

Founded in 1976 and has always focused on education and providing information, particularly to municipalities, organisations and authorities. Interest in veganism in Sweden has increased greatly, especially among young people during the last few years. The Society sells national and international literature on veganism.

Svenska Vegetariska Föreningen
(Vegetarian Society Sweden)
Sågargatan 4
S-116 36 Stockholm
Tel: +46-8-702 11 16, Fax: +46-8-702 11 17
email: svf@vegetarian.se, Website: www.vegetarian.se
Magazine: Vegetar four times a year.

The Vegetarian Society (Sweden) was founded in 1903 and will celebrate its 100th anniversary in 2003 by hosting the European Vegetarian Union (EVU) Congress. Every 1st October, World Vegetarian Day, the society, together with the Swedish Vegan Sociey and Animal Rights Sweden, organises seminars, vegetarian cooking competitions and exhibitions. The Vegetarian Society aims to inform and inspire people to adopt a healthy vegetarian lifestyle, mainly through giving advice by telephone, its quarterly magazine and lectures.

Föreningen Justa Bananer
Lunda Vägen 62
23252 Åkard
Tel: +46-40-461682
www.algonet.se/~tyling/   email: jbanana@ivu.org

For groups in other countries you can find links from these sites:

Animal Contacts Directory www.veggies.org.uk

International Vegetarian Union www.ivu.org

European Vegetarian Union www.ivu.org/evu

VEGETARIAN BRITAIN

The complete day out, weekend and holiday guide.

Over 100 hotels and guest houses.

Hundreds of vegetarian restaurants and cafes. Detailed descriptions with opening times and full price details.

Whats on the menu for Vegans?

Perfect for veggies and those who love them... (or'd like to)

The most comprehensive Vegetarian Guide ever printed!

Foreword by Paul and Linda McCartney

By Alex Bourke and Alan Todd

500 places to eat and sleep including 80 veggie guest houses. Ideal for weekends away for burned out activists.

£7.99

150 places to eat and sleep, including large Paris section and country bed and breakfasts.

£6.99

100 veggie restaurants in London listing what's on the menu for vegans. Plus 150 wholefood and health food stores. Perfect for foraging while on a demo or visiting.

£5.99

www.vegetarianguides.com

The time is always ripe

to do right

chapter seventeen

AND FINALLY...

The vast majority of people who get involved in campaigning work are genuine, honest and compassionate. Unfortunately, for every ten of these genuine people you meet, there is likely to be one person whose motives are not as honourable.

We have had personal experience of people who get involved in animal rights purely for their own benefit. The problem is, it takes a while to get to know someone properly and a person can join a local group and take advantage of your trust, then leave before you discover the damage they've done.

We have heard of instances when money and equipment has "gone missing" from stalls and offices. Large 0898 phone bills were run up by a campaigner who was "dog sitting" for another campaigner, and vehicle offences have been committed by drivers of vehicles bought for group use.

There are also people who join groups purely as a method of gaining an instant circle of friends, pretend to be vegetarian or even vegan, then drop out of the group suddenly after falling out with someone else there. Such people can be vindictive, spreading rumours and setting people up against each other.

It's important to be careful, but not too careful. Mistrust and paranoia can be just as damaging to the stability of your group as dishonest members.

Just take precautions when new members join, confirm their addresses and don't encourage them to fundraise by themselves or give them access to money or equipment belonging to the group until you've got to know them better.

There is another kind of potential troublemaker who is more of a nuisance than a danger, the disruptive, angry, but genuinely committed vegan who is always trying to start arguments with other group members. They don't seem to understand that persuasion gets people up and active but patronising just gets up their nose.

Usually this type is after attention and can be controlled by the group sticking together if he or she tries to intimidate quieter members. (After a divorce and being sacked and a few years of therapy some of them change into really nice people, but there again, some don't !)

The very significant successes of the animal rights movement have happened because many diverse groups of people are prepared to work together, putting aside personal differences in the name of unity.

You will be amazed at what a small number of committed people can do. But don't just take our word for it...

ABOUT THE AUTHORS

Ronny is in her late twenties. Her main aim in life is to help capture the hearts and minds of the nation and steer them along the vegan path by any means possible. She is rarely far from a computer and writes books whenever she gets the chance.

Ronny has lived in various parts of Britain, gaining 'on the streets' experience through working with lots of other campaigners. She has written various booklets and leaflets as well as articles for several magazines, and she has appeared on radio and television.

Ronny believes that an active network of local groups and clued-up, inspired individuals is the best way to spread awareness of animal abuse and bring about lasting change. She likes researching, developing, (and especially testing) new vegan cake recipes, as well as reading, art, walking, and general frivolity. When she retires, she plans to run a guinea pig sanctuary.

Alex was born in 1961 and has lived and campaigned in Britain, France and Poland, including a year working at Viva! He founded Vegetarian Guides Ltd to map the world for vegans and is a member of the Vegan Society Council. He wrote or co-wrote The Vegan Guide to Paris, The Hippy Cookbook, How to Write a Vegan Book, Vegetarian London, Vegetarian France, Vegetarian Britain and Vegetarian Europe.

He believes world veganization will be achieved by empowering local activists with first class campaigning materials. He speaks several languages and loves to go backpacking loaded with subversive vegan literature, sparking alliances between groups and having loads of fun. His writing workshops at vegan festivals have resulted in many new books.

Having given up his former life as a software engineer, he still lives with two computers.

With grateful thanks to the following people and groups for help or inspiration:

David Lane
Robin Lane
Neil Lea
Andrew Butler, Tracy Reiman, Toni Vernelli and
Anna West at PETA
Patrick Smith
Elizabeth Wolf
Clare
Jon Hindle

Des Murphy & Co solicitors, Brighton
Tim Walker of Walkers Solicitors for writing Chapter 13
Andrew Richards for helping with the website
London Animal Action
Veggies Catering Campaign

Harry Snell at Innervision for editing and co-producing the video of the book (see inside back cover) and PETA for supporting it

Special thanks to Mark Halunga (markmail@chello.se), who did the front cover illustration, and Marion Gillet who coordinated design of the cover. Marion, as a veggie designer, will be happy to consider any "design against cruelty" and can be contacted at mariongb@hotmail.com.

FEEDBACK

Like what you've read? Please tell everyone!

Don't like something or have updates or improvements?
Please note them here and tell us!

Scamp Media
PO Box 2284
London W1A 5UH
England

www.scampsite.co.uk

Thanks!

Knowledge is power ... so share it!

TO ORDER MORE COPIES OF THIS BOOK

Individual copies of this book can be obtained by sending a UK cheque or postal order for £4.99 payable to "Vegetarian Guides" to:

Scamp Media
PO Box 2284
London W1A 5UH

www.scampsite.co.uk

Credit card and overseas orders to
www.vegetarianguides.com

TRADE ORDERS

Mail, fax or email your order or enquiry to:

Vegetarian Guides Ltd
PO Box 2284
London W1A 5UH

Fax 0870-121 4721
International Fax +44-870-121 4721
info@vegetarianguides.com

Get these books out and change the world!
Discounts available for animal rights groups
and campaigning organisations.

ADVERTISERS INDEX

ALF SG — 116

Animal Aid — 12

Animal Rights Coalition (ARCNews) — 22

Animal Rights (video) — inside back cover

The Cake Scoffer, by Ronny — 132

Compassion in World Farming — inside front cover

Ethical Wares — 14

London Animal Action — 32

People for the Ethical Treatment of Animals — 17

Stop Huntingdon Animal Cruelty — 31

Uncaged Campaigns — 27

Vegetarian Guides — 182

Walkers Solicitors — 131

SUCCESS

It is not the position you stand,

but the direction in which you look